OHAFFIA

A MATRILINEAL IBO PEOPLE

PHILIP O. NSUGBE

OXFORD
AT THE CLARENDON PRESS
1974

Oxford University Press, Ely House, London W. 1

GLASGOW NEW YORK TORONTO MELBOURNE WELLINGTON
CAPE TOWN IBADAN NAIROBI DAR ES SALAAM LUSAKA ADDIS ABABA
DELHI BOMBAY CALCUTTA MADRAS KARACHI LAHORE DACCA
KUALA LUMPUR SINGAPORE HONG KONG TOKYO

ISBN 0 19 823182 2

© *Oxford University Press 1974*

*Printed in Great Britain
at the University Press, Oxford
by Vivian Ridler
Printer to the University*

PREFACE

THE eight million or so Ibo of the Federation of Nigeria live mainly to the east of the lower Niger, with a smaller extension of some 250,000 on the west bank.[1] In addition to inhabiting a compact stretch of territory, the Ibo speak a common language and can be said to possess, in good measure, similar social systems. Because of the broad similarities of their culture, they have been described by Forde and Jones as a single people.[2] However, to stress these cultural similarities might lead one to underestimate the differences which a close study of the main groupings of the Ibo discloses. When therefore the Ibo are discussed, as they must be, on the basis of these groupings, such differences as those of dialect and social institutions become much more significant.

In this study I shall try to contribute to the existing knowledge of the Ibo in terms of some of their differences. I shall examine certain aspects of the social system of a selected Ibo community, the Ohaffia, for the purpose.

The Ohaffia Ibo and five other Ibo communities have been grouped by Forde and Jones into one main category which they have called the Cross River Ibo. This grouping is one of five such groupings into which the Ibo have been divided.[3] The territories occupied by the Cross River Ibo communities lie immediately to the west of the Cross River. These communities show considerable contrast in their culture and social organization with the other four main Ibo groupings. For the purposes of the present study, I shall refer to these other four main groupings as the 'general Ibo'.[4] This usage admittedly begs a number of questions, but I use it to be able to indicate the contrast between the Cross River Ibo and

[1] The disputed Federal Census of December 1963, published in February 1964, put the population of Eastern Nigeria at 12·5 million. At the 1966 Constitutional Conference, the Western Nigeria Delegation put the Eastern Nigeria Ibo at 7·8 million. The Ibo of the Mid-west Region of Nigeria are generally stated to be just over 250,000.

[2] D. Forde and G. I. Jones, *The Ibo and the Ibibio-speaking Peoples of South-Eastern Nigeria*, Oxford University Press for the International African Institute, 1950, p. 9.   [3] Forde and Jones, 1950, p. 10.

[4] These others are Northern or Onitsha Ibo, Southern or Owerri Ibo, Western Ibo, and North-Eastern Ibo (ibid.).

the picture of the 'Ibo' generally gained from the standard works of Meek as well as Forde and Jones.[5]

The differences between the Cross River Ibo and the so-called 'general Ibo' lie most obviously in their systems of kinship and marriage, in their rules of inheritance and succession, and in the forms of their men's associations and cults.[6] For example, whereas 'patrilineal' systems predominate among the 'general Ibo', 'matrilineal' elements (which are even stated by some authors to be essentially 'non-Ibo')[7] predominate in the social systems of the Cross River Ibo (the Aro Ibo, in this grouping, being the only exception).

These differences have been known to exist for some time by ethnographers. G. T. Basden, one of the best-known of the earlier students of the Ibo, and probably the first to mention that matriliny existed in some form among the Ibo, said in this connection: 'I know of but one part of Ibo country where matrilineal succession is the accepted order and that is among the Ohaffia towns (a little north of Aro-Chuku). It is strange to meet with this apparently isolated example.'[8]

Up to now detailed studies made of the Ibo have dealt exclusively with the 'general Ibo'.[9] None has been published on any of the Cross River Ibo communities. The Ohaffia material provided in the present study is therefore meant in some measure to make good the omission.

Chapters I and II of the study provide a general introductory picture of Ohaffia people through their habitat and economy, and also through one or two other topics relevant to the understanding of the people and their social system. The abridged version of their oral tradition of origin given in Chapter I reveals how the people attempt to explain the sources of certain social phenomena in their culture. In the place of some of these traditions and 'onomastic' tales[10] I have sometimes suggested alternative anthropological explanations.

[5] The works referred to here are C. K. Meek, *Law and Authority among a Nigerian Tribe*, London, 1937; and Forde and Jones, 1950.
[6] Forde and Jones, 1950, p. 52.   [7] Ibid.
[8] G. T. Basden, *The Niger Ibos*, London, 1938 (reprinted 1966), p. 268. A similar reference is also made by Forde and Jones, p. 52.
[9] A further example is M. M. Green, *Ibo Village Affairs*, London, 1947.
[10] E. W. Ardener, 'Documentary and Linguistic Evidence for the Rise of the Trading Polities between Rio Del Rey and Cameroons, 1500–1650', *History and Social Anthropology*, A.S.A. Monograph No. 7, London, 1968.

In Chapters III to IX, I deal mainly with those features of the Ohaffia social system which show significant contrasts with those of any known groups among the 'general Ibo'. Chapter X attempts to relate the data presented in earlier parts of the study to some current theoretical positions on the phenomenon of matriliny and on rules of descent and descent-groups. In the final chapter some recent changes in the society are discussed.

Most of the ethnographic material upon which the study is based was collected in Ohaffia country in the course of my duties as government ethnographer and antiquities officer from November 1960 to August 1962 from my station at Oron on the Cross River estuary, some 120 miles by land south of Ohaffia.

The study is a general one indicating the main areas of significant cultural differences between the Ohaffia and the 'general Ibo'. In this sense the contribution is new to the existing ethnographic literature on the Ibo. I know the Ohaffia people and their country fairly well. I revisited certain parts of the country in August 1964 and in September 1965.

ACKNOWLEDGEMENTS

THE writing of this monograph was completed towards the end of 1967 for the Oxford University B.Litt. By this time the effects of the Nigerian civil war, now well into its second year, were beginning to take their inexorable toll on my finances and disposition to work. The point of this statement lies in its link with the part that Linacre (my college at Oxford) and my friends played in enabling me to complete my writing. I am indebted to my college, particularly to Mr. J. B. Bamborough, its Principal, and to Dr. R. Cecil, its Vice-Principal, for their active promotion of my case for grants from the University Chest.

To Mr. A. D. Hazlewood, Fellow of Pembroke College, Oxford, and his wife, to Mrs. Patricia St.-Johns, formerly Manageress of Summertown House, my sincere thanks for their deep interest in my family and in the progress of my work in those difficult times. To Dr. D. F. Mullins, Mr. Heinz E. Kiewe, Professor J. H. M. Beattie, and others I am unable to name here, my thanks for their friendship.

I have acknowledgements of a different order to make to others with respect to the practical task of producing the monograph. To Mr. B. E. B. Fagg, O.B.E., Fellow of Linacre College, Oxford, I owe my first opportunity in direct fieldwork experience. As Director and Head of the Department of Antiquities and the National Museums of Nigeria, he urged me as an inexperienced government ethnographer to push out into the field to work. My Ohaffia material was largely collected then.

To Agwu Mba, Chief Uduma, and the late Chief Inspector Ama, all of Ohaffia, for serving me as guides and informants in the field; to Uga Onwuka and Abasi and their wives (my Ohaffia friends in Oxford) my thanks for helping to sort out my facts about their people.

To Professor (now Sir) Edward Evans-Pritchard, then Head of the Institute of Social Anthropology, Oxford, who invited me to Oxford years before I was free to come, and to his secretary Miss Barbara Allaway, I owe the privileges of access to the vast sources of reference and facilities at the Institute. I make special mention here of Sir Edward Evans-Pritchard's magnanimity.

But it is to Mr. Edwin Ardener of St. John's College, Oxford, and the Institute of Social Anthropology that I am particularly indebted for guidance in the organization of my field-material as well as for directing my search to sources hitherto unknown to me. His uncanny grasp of Ibo life-style, being also himself a remarkable Ibo scholar, cannot escape mention.

To Dr. Phyllis Kaberry of London University, Dr. Audrey Butt (now Mrs. Colson), Fellow of St. Hugh's College, Oxford, to my colleague and friend, Professor H. J. Simons of the University of Zambia, I owe sincere gratitude for their encouragement to publish this study.

The claims of my wife, Chukwunyem, to credit are of course indisputable. For all the errors of writing in a foreign language I hold no one else but myself responsible.

P. O. N.

CONTENTS

LIST OF MAPS

LIST OF FIGURES

LIST OF TABLES

A NOTE ON ORTHOGRAPHY

As Ibo orthography has been modified from time to time, it is difficult to be certain of the version in current use. In view of this, I have kept as close as possible to the Bible orthography (the so-called 'Old Orthography'), which is still the one that most literate Ibos are familiar with.

Some guide to Ibo tone-markings is provided below:

i. High tones are left unmarked, as in *ogo*, meaning 'an open meeting-place'.
ii. Low tones are marked thus ['], as in *àgà*, meaning 'barren woman'.
iii. Mid tones are marked ['], as in *nkità*, meaning 'dog'.
iv. After a mid tone marked as in (iii) above, the absence of tone-marks represents a continuation of the same level, as in *nye m ihe* meaning 'give me something'.

Ibo terms are marked for tones as well as being italicized. The spelling of Ibo place-names follows the common usage in maps.

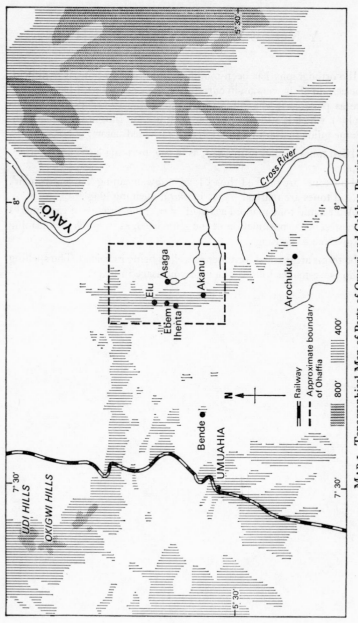

MAP I. Topographical Map of Parts of Owerri and Calabar Provinces

I

THE LAND, PEOPLE, AND TRADITION
OF ORIGIN

Ohaffia: Location, Size, and Topography

THE Cross River Ibo grouping comprises the Ohaffia and five other Ibo communities.[1] These others are the *Nkporo Adà* to the north of the *Ohaffia*, the *Ihè* and the *Arò* to the south, the *Abàm* to the south-west, and the *Abiriba* to the west. The territories of these communities, including the Ohaffia, mark the geographical frontier of Iboland in the east.[2]

Ohaffia itself is located closest to the river, on a 'hoe-shaped' ridge at the extreme north-north-eastern corner of the Bende Division. It has an estimated area of 110 square miles, bounded approximately by latitudes 5° 30' and 5° 45' north, and longitudes 7° 45' and 7° 55' east. The portion of the ridge within Ohaffia runs through the heart of the country from north to south.[3] But the bulk of it is seen to veer directly westward from Ohaffia and to run in that direction for some 50 miles before turning north to form the Okigwi-Udi group of hills.[4] Continuing north, it broadens out, then merges finally with the dissected northward-rising plain which traverses the northern half of Southern Nigeria from west to east.

The landscape of this portion of Eastern Nigeria has been described by Kitson as 'a strip of country about 80 miles long and 5 to 20 miles broad consisting of sedimentary rocks of Cretaceous and Late Tertiary Age. It forms the Okigwi-Udi-Urukuram highlands which extend from the Northern Nigeria border southwards beyond Okigwi and forms the watershed between the Niger and the

---

[1] See p. v of the Preface.

[2] See Map 4. The *Ihè* and the *Ututù* (the latter not mentioned in the text) are generally referred to as *Abàm*. This grouping has been ignored because it is rather arbitrary.

[3] See Map 1 in which Ohaffia territory is approximately marked out in broken lines.

[4] See Map 1.

Cross River. Its altitude from south to north varies from 700 feet
to 2,000 feet above sea-level.'[5]

Numerous streams flank both the eastern and the western sides
of the Ohaffia ridge. The streams to the east eventually empty
into the south-flowing Cross River, the largest but one of Eastern
Nigeria's rivers. To the west, the streams are fewer but relatively
longer. These drain first into the Uduma which flows directly
south to join the Igwu and the Inyang rivers to form the Enyong
Creek.[6] The Enyong and the Cross discharge into the Gulf of
Guinea through the Calabar Estuary, formerly the main gateway
into Eastern Nigeria until the opening of Port Harcourt in the
first decade of the present century.

Thus Ohaffia is a moderately hilly and well-watered country,
and although it is broken in places by narrow and steep-sided
valleys, the landscape on the whole is not harsh to the eye.[7] The
moderate elevation of the country[8] barely raises it above the
swampy lowlands in the neighbourhood, but it is sufficient to
make the country relatively open to breezes, and therefore health-
ier and free from insect pests—a natural advantage which made
Ohaffia the choice of the United Free Church of Scotland when
this Mission opened in 1911, one of the first and most important
centres of Christian activity in Eastern Nigeria despite its situation
in quite a remote[9] part of Iboland.

Accessibility and Routes

Even today Ohaffia is still relatively isolated and difficult of
access from most directions. In the east, the approach is from the
thickly forested Cross River Valley, and is still further blocked by
the Cameroon mountain wall. In the south is a low-lying swampy
country, although once the Cross River is reached, it offers the
easiest and quickest way out of Ohaffia but in a direction away
from the heart of Ibo country.

Ironically, the easiest land route leading into Ohaffia and out of
it was the one factor that isolated the country most from the main

[5] A. E. Kitson, 'Southern Nigeria: Some Considerations of its Structure,
People and Natural History', *Geographical Journal*, xli (Jan.-June 1913), 18.
[6] J. S. Harris, 'Papers on the Economic Aspect of Life among the Ozuitem
Ibo', *Africa*, xiv (Jan. 1943), 12–13.
[7] See Pl. I.   [8] At its highest point Ohaffia is 463 feet above sea-level.
[9] J. C. Mayne, 'Memorandum, Ref. No. OW. 873/31, 22/1/34, to Ag. Resident, Owerri Province, Port Harcourt', National Archives, Enugu, E. Nigeria.

Ibo cultural area. This is the route along the crest of the ridge
which we have already seen to be relatively high and dry and not
thickly forested. For non-riverain people like the Ohaffia, movement
along this highland route would be relatively easier and safer. The
difficulty again was that it ran roughly from north to south like the
Cross River, away from the heart of Iboland. However, it must be
one of the oldest routes in this region.[10]

It may well be true that the Efik and other Ibibio-speaking
peoples used the Cross and the Enyong rivers as their main high-
ways of movement in earlier times, as they claim in their accounts
of their migrations.[11] The attempt in 1841 by Captain Becroft
(later better known as Beecroft) to penetrate the region by going
up the Cross River failed.[12] The only successful penetrations
made later by the British military expeditions and the Christian
Missions, and later still by modern commerce, reached Ohaffia
and the surrounding country not by going up the Cross River but
through the highland route.

The activities of the Aro Chuku 'Long Juju' during and after
the period of slave trade, about which we shall hear later, are
traditionally said to have been carried on, at least in part, along the
highland route. It is also likely that the route had linked Aro
Chuku (located directly on the southern tip of Ohaffia ridge) with
Northern Nigeria. If so, it certainly passed through Ohaffia to
Okigwi, Udi, and Awka, and also to Nsukka and through Nsukka
to Idah on the Niger, and probably also joining the main trans-
Saharan slave routes from Idah. Aro Chuku was the notorious
centre of the slave trade in this region. Because of this role 'the
Aro Field Force was organized at Old Calabar, and a short but
sharp campaign of three months sufficed to put an end to it'.[13]

Old men who in their manhood served as government load-
carriers, or as mission teachers, cooks, and stewards during the
opening up of the country early in this century, and others too
who were recruited to work as labourers during the building of the

[10] Forde and Jones, 1950, p. 52.
[11] A. K. Hart, *Report of the Inquiry into the Dispute over Obongship of Calabar*,
Enugu, 1964, p. 25.
[12] Capt. Becroft, 'On Benin and the Upper Course of the River Quorra, or
Niger', as communicated by Robert Jamieson in the *Journal of the Royal Geographical Society of London*, xi (1841), 189–90.
[13] D. A. MacAlister, 'The Aro Country, Southern Nigeria', *Scottish Geographical Magazine*, xviii (Dec. 1902), 634. The Aro Expedition referred to here took
place in 1901; cf. Meek, 1937, p. 44 n.

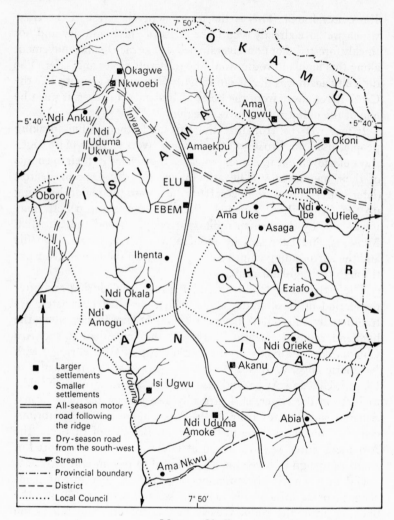

MAP 2. Ohaffia

Eastern Nigeria railway, were still able to recall their long marches through the upland paths—mostly during the night so as to avoid the exhausting noonday heat.

The traditional links of friendship among the Ohaffia, the Ada, and the Aro peoples in joint military and trade activities before the coming of the British (a friendship still cherished by them today and about which we shall hear more later) obviously had a topographical basis to it. Today the best approach to Ohaffia is still by the modern motor-road which follows the ridge through Ohaffia to Aro Chuku.

In contrast to this highland route, there is another which leads direct from the south-west through Bende town into Ohaffia.[14] As an alternative route to Ohaffia, its use remains a risky undertaking even when the season is dry. During the rains it becomes virtually unusable. This approach is also marked by bad curves, deep ravines, and swamps right from Umuahia township through Bende to Ohaffia itself. Thus the very difficult terrain has rendered the route not only tedious but dangerous. This difficulty in part explains the decline of Bende town, formerly the Administrative Headquarters of the Division which still bears its name. Now Umuahia, a main route town, has supplanted Bende.

Vegetation and Animal Life

In the main, the vegetation cover of Ohaffia country can be described as 'orchard bush',[15] a cross between forest and savanna. Like other parts of the Okigwi-Udi-Urukuram highlands, Ohaffia is 'for the most part open and well-grassed with patches of light forest on the hills and thicker vegetation in the valleys'.[16] The groves of big trees which can still be seen in the open landscape suggest that before the effects of shifting cultivation and erosion from slope-farming combined with the pressure of a growing population, high forest may have been extensive over the ridge. The existence in Ohaffia of old artefacts such as big war-drums, huge ritual posts ornately carved,[17] and massive fetish figures

---

[14] See Map 2.
[15] Intelligence Report on Ohaffia Clan, 1931, National Archives, Enugu, Eastern Nigeria. See also Pl. I.
[16] MacAlister, 1902, p. 630.
[17] Now officially called 'Ohaffia Posts' by the National Museum of Nigeria. See Fig. 10.

carved in wood, may also support the notion that the country was more wooded than it is at the present time.[18]

To the south and east, barely beyond Ohaffia territory, thick forest is still in almost complete dominance. Now in selected areas, such as Itu Mbauzo and Amaeke Abam, farm-settlement projects by the Regional Government for school-leavers are being launched. Bulldozers and caterpillars have been busy in the drier and more open valleys churning out acres of virgin farmland.

Cash-crop plantations are becoming increasingly fashionable, especially for Ohaffia businessmen and others who are indigenous to the area but living outside. Such people are in a position to find the capital more readily than some of their village relatives at home. Retired civil servants and old mission teachers, for example, are taking to plantation-farming though on a small scale. They grow new breeds of oil-palm, cocoa, and rubber trees, with the help and advice of the Agricultural College at Umudike some five miles from Umuahia township.

Good and valuable timber, mainly mahogany, iroko (*Chlorophora excelsa*), camwood (*Baphia nitida*), and others less useful, such as the silk-cotton tree (*Ceiba pentandra*), are still to be found in the more forested parts to the east and south just beyond Ohaffia country. But these are still difficult to reach and to exploit. Economic trees are generally semi-wild. They include oil palm (*Elaeis guineensis*), raffia palm (*Raphia vinifera*), coconut (*Cocos nucifera*), native pear (*Pachylobus edulis*), African bread fruit (*Treculia africana*), wild mango (*Irvingia gabonensis*), mango (*Mangifera indica*), cola (*Cola acuminata*), papaw (*Carica papaya*), sweet orange (*Citrus aurantium*), lime (*Citrus medica*, var. *acida*), and sugar cane (*Saccharum officinarum*). The food staples are yam (*Dioscorea spp.*), mainly of the white and the yellow varieties, and bitter yam (*Dioscorea bulbifera*), cassava (*Manihot utilissima*), cocoyam (*Colocasia esculenta*),[19] rice (*Oryza sativa*), eaten, but not grown, plantain (*Musa sapientum*, var. *paradisiaca*), banana (*Musa sapientum*), maize or corn (*Zea mays*), pumpkins (*Cucurbitaceae*) both of the calabash family and the fluted pumpkin (*Telfairea occidentalis*), water melon (*Citrullus vulgaris*), and native bean (*akidi* in Ibo) or cow pea (*Vigna unguiculata*). Some of the vegetable

---

[18] Traditionally Ohaffia was a crafts centre. It was unlikely therefore that wood for carving was purchased.

[19] New to the Ohaffia economy and not popular as food staple.

staple spinach are bitter leaf, *aṅàra miri* (*Entada abyssinica*), cucumber (*Cucumis sativus*), okro (*Hibiscus esculentus*), garden egg (*Solanum melongena*), tomato (*Lycopersicum esculentum*), mushroom, *àchàrà* (*Pennisetum purpureum*), *utazìzì*, *ugu*, *ṅzìma*, Indian spinach (*Basella alba*), black pepper (*Piper nigrum*), Chile pepper (*Capsicum frutescens*), and a few other kinds. No groundnuts are planted.

Wildlife is now rare. Its absence is an index of growing population pressure upon food resources, but it is still said to include the leopard, bush-hog (sacred to certain Ohaffia lineages), antelope, deer, and bush-fowl. The cane-rat ('cutting-grass'), squirrel, bush-rat, bat, and snail are still to be found, and many of these are hunted or collected for food. Livestock consists mainly of fowl, goat, and pig; the last two are usually found tethered or restricted because, in places, farms and gardens are within village lands. Cattle are not kept at all. Sheep are rare. Goats are mainly used for ritual purposes, and generally but not exclusively owned and kept by the women.

Rainfall

Annual rainfall is not likely to be less than 50 inches or to exceed 85,[20] but no records have been kept or at least are available. It is not possible therefore to give an exact average annual measure for the area. Driving rains occur, and this explains in part why the mud and wattle huts are built low with the eaves of the thatched roofs wide and quite close to the ground.

Population: Size and Distribution

The Ohaffia are administratively, although incorrectly, still referred to as a 'clan'. In the 1930s and earlier, government officials used the term 'clan' to refer to distinctive groups of villages within one main language-group (or 'tribe').[21] The usage was not confined to Eastern Nigeria but was also common in parts of present-day Midwestern and Northern Nigeria as well as the Cameroons. The term has since stuck, and a good many ethnic and administrative sub-groups, even now, are still officially called 'clans'.

[20] W. B. Morgan and R. P. Moss, 'Savanna and Forest in Western Nigeria', *Africa*, xxxv (July 1965), 286–94, for an idea of the rain-belt in which Ohaffia country lies.
[21] J. S. Harris quotes P. A. Talbot as being the first to use the term 'clan' incorrectly. Later administrative officials copied Talbot; see Harris, 1943, p. 12.

Of the twenty-five villages that comprise the Ohaffia Ibo, all but one share a tradition of common descent. Ihenta, the exception, of obscure origin, is acknowledged by the rest of Ohaffia villages as distinct, and to have existed before the migration of the latter into their present territory. Until about 1934, this little village,

TABLE 1(*a*). *Population Figures of Ohaffia Villages**

Isiama Ohaffia (30,681)		Ohafor Ohaffia (13,617)		Okamu Ohaffia (9,801)	
Ebem	11,114	Asaga	8,043	Okoni	5,882
Amaekpu	9,398	Eziafor	2,367	Amangwu	2,422
Elu	4,357	Amuke/Ndi Ibe	2,241	Amuma	1,160
Okagwe	3,357	Ndi Orieke	966	Ufiele	337
Nkwoebi	1,388				
Ndi Anku	623				
Oboro	444				
Ihenta†					
Ndi Okala†					
Ndi Amogu†					
Ndi Uduma Ukwu†					

TABLE 1(*b*). *Estimates for Villages in Ania Ohaffia not mentioned in the Delimitation Report*

Ania Ohaffia (15,150)	
Akanu	12,000
Isi Ugwu	1,500
Ndi Uduma Awoke	1,500
Abia	75
Amankwu	75

* Source: *Report of the Constituency Delimitation Commission,* 1964, except for villages in Ania Ohaffia which are estimated in Table 1(*b*) above.

† Four villages merged with bigger villages by the Delimitation Commission.

with a population then of twenty-nine adults,[22] had held itself aloof from the others. But with the establishment of the British Administration in 1934, the village was allowed, by its own wish, to join with the Ohaffia proper to form one Local County Council.[23]

The population figures for Ohaffia villages are not complete in any single available source of information. The figures for the villages in three of the four local council units into which Ohaffia

[22] J. C. Mayne, op. cit.   [23] Ibid.

has recently been divided,[24] are given in Table 1(*a*) as recorded in the *Report of the Constituency Delimitation Commission* of 1964.[25] For the five villages in Ania Ohaffia (the fourth local council unit not included in this report), I have estimated their population as shown in Table 1(*b*) so as to complete the data. Ohaffia is part of the larger District Council area of Owuwa Anyanwu. It is possible, as has happened in the past, that the five villages in Ania Ohaffia were placed in another constituency by the Commission[26] solely for political convenience or as thought fit by it. In estimating the population of the five villages, I have used the following aids: (i) older estimates from such sources as Forde and Jones;[27] (ii) my estimates guided sometimes by local opinion about the sizes of the villages concerned; and (iii) hints in the official map about the relative importance of the villages.[28]

Thus Akanu in Table 1(*b*), locally regarded as the most populous of the Ohaffia villages, has been estimated by me at 12,000, a little higher than Ebem in Table 1(*a*) the population of which is known. Akanu is also listed first by Forde and Jones with *Asaga*, *Okon* (Okoni), Amaekpu, and Ebem among settlements 'of from 3,000 to 5,000 people', in 1935–40.[29] That Akanu would have had to double in population in the generation since then to approach my total of 12,000 is not out of line with Nigerian demographic performance.

Two other villages, Isi Ugwu and Ndi Uduma Awoke, in the same unit as Akanu in Table 1(*b*), are all about the same size as each other and I estimate them to be 1,500 each at least. The two villages thus would total 3,000 people. The two remaining villages

---

[24] See Chapter III for a detailed discussion of the four units.

[25] The disputed figures of the 1963 census were made available to the Delimitation Commission only, under the chairmanship of E. E. Esua, which completed the enormous task in six weeks. In 1958, a similar commission chaired by Lord Merthyr, took six months to complete the same task. Thus there was the element of rush in the work of the Esua Commission due to pressure imposed upon it by political interests.

[26] Such transfers have occurred in the past. In 1954, 'a transfer of 4,801 people from *Elu Elu* District to Ikot Ekpene Division' was made regardless of the ethnic origin of the persons transferred. The 1958 Delimitation Commission admitted having toyed with the idea of linking 'the whole of Owuwa Anyanwu District Council Area (comprising Abiriba, Nkporo Ada, Abam, and Ohaffia) with the District Area of the Arò/Ibo in Enyong Division' in Ibibio country (see the *Report of the Constituency Delimitation Commission*, 1958, p. 71).

[27] Forde and Jones, 1950, p. 54.

[28] See Map 2.   [29] Forde and Jones, 1950, p. 54.

of Abia and Amankwu in Table 1(*b*) are very small, little more than farm settlements, and very much smaller than Ufiele (pop. 337). I have assigned them an arbitrary figure of 75 each which seems to me not seriously to over-estimate their populations.

In Table 1(*a*) the villages of Ihenta, Ndi Amogu, Ndi Okala, and Ndi Uduma Ukwu are known to consist of not more than two or three huts each, and to be largely farm settlements (as often happens in these areas where farms are located far from the owning groups). They were considered to be too small to appear independently in the Delimitation Report and were merged with bigger villages. The report does not specify these but they probably are the settlements nearest them or those with which they have traditional links. Thus Ihenta I take to be linked with Ebem because of their proximity, and similarly Ndi Okala and Ndi Amogu with Ebem. Ndi Uduma Ukwu I link with Elu to which it is ritually and economically related.

Thus, adding up the totals of Tables 1 (*a*) and (*b*), the population of the Ohaffia would be in the order of 69,000. A crude check on this figure could be worked out by a different method. Forde and Jones gave the approximate number of *active adult males* of the Ohaffia in 1935–40 as 6,200.[30] If this is multiplied by a factor of four, we arrive at a late 1930s figure of 24,800 for the total population. Once more the population would have had to more than double in twenty-five years to reach my estimate of 69,000 for the 1960s. Given the unreliability of early tax figures and the high fertility rates known for Eastern Nigeria, I am informed that these figures are not impossible.

As further check, the relative sizes of many of the Ohaffia villages can also be independently guessed from the official map reproduced here as Map 2. Six of the seven villages described in the Delimitation Report as large (3,000 or over) are also shown in the map as 'larger settlements'.[31] The only discrepancy in this connection is Asaga whose population is shown in Table 1(*a*) to be large, which my own visits confirm, but is not so marked in the official map.[32]

Similarly, many of the villages shown by the report's figures to have less than 3,000 people are also represented as small in the map. There are three villages, namely Isi Ugwu, Ndi Uduma Awoke, and Nkwoebi, which appear on the map as larger settlements but are shown in the table as small. The official map, it must be remembered, does not give its criteria for size. However, such villages as Ihenta, Ndi Okala, and Ndi Uduma Ukwu are known, as we have earlier stated, to number fewer than 50 people each, while Asaga, on the other hand, is known to run to about 8,000.

Now taking a conservative estimate of 65,000 to be the population of Ohaffia in the 1960s, we arrive at a population density of over 500. This is heavy for a rural area. But it still presents a false picture of the true population distribution over the territory, as it does not reflect the heavy pressure on land-use in certain parts of Ohaffia. For example, the six villages with a population of more than 3,000 each, representing over 75 per cent of the total population of Ohaffia, are sited, as can be seen from Map 2, on the ridge which in places is less than five miles across. Thus most people in Ohaffia are concentrated in a belt of high population density. This is reflected in the compactness of housing pattern in any of the six ridge-villages. Another five of the smaller villages are also sited on the ridge. The low-lying areas in Ohaffia are broken, fissured, not everywhere suitable for habitation, and hardly usable for agriculture. Farming land can therefore be said to be scarce, and such as is available is often situated some distance away from the owning-groups, or from the houses of the villagers using them. This is specially true of the villages on the ridge, particularly the larger ones.[33]

The Name 'Ohaffia'

The name 'Ohaffia' (correctly: *Ọhaafia'*) is made up of two Ibo words: *ọhà*, 'people' (in some contexts to be interpreted as 'warriors'), and a word interpreted either as *ọfia*, 'forest', or *afia*, 'market'.

Three meanings are thus possible: (i) *Ọhà-ọfia*: 'people of the forest', a name that an Ibo people is unlikely to ascribe to itself, because of its pejorative overtones; (ii) *Ọhà-ọfia*: with the alternative meanings: 'warriors of the forest' or, more to the point,

---

[33] *Amaekpu* village-farmlands are up to six or seven miles away to the northwest of the village, off the ridge motor-way.

'guerilla warriors'[34] (the Ohaffia were dreaded mercenaries of the Aro, as we shall see); and (iii) *Ọhà-afia*, an abbreviation implying 'Can a whole people or village (*ọhà*) go to market (*afia*) *at this time of night?*' This is what tradition insists is the true meaning of the name. It will become clearer when we come to discuss the Ohaffia tradition of origin.

There is also an additional dimension in meaning and usage to the word *ọhà* among the Ibo which imparts the dynamism of 'motion', 'voice', or 'power' to the word. Thus *ọhà* in motion may well be an angry body of citizens protesting against, or urging for, a particular course of action. *Ọhà* can also refer to a body of men in authority, for example a government; or it can mean the force of public opinion. The individual Ibo man often considers himself to be powerless against *ọha*—a powerlessness that is widely acknowledged in Ibo personal names and in Ibo proverbs. Such personal names generally imply a protest against this power. For example, *Ọnuọhà*, a personal name which means, as it stands here, 'voice of people', may, in full, end in one of a number of forms to mean a number of things which the 'voice' of the people, it is wished, may or may not do to the individual, thus *Ọnu ọhà egbùlam* (literally, 'voice of people, do not kill me'). One can also think of a number of Ibo proverbs which imply the immense and overwhelming weight of *ọha*, and the folly of opposing it.

The Ohaffia and their Neighbours

The Ohaffia belong to one of the four head-hunting warrior communities in the Bende Division. The others are the Ada, the Abam, and the Abiriba. Although, no doubt, a good number of other Ibo communities were also in the past formidable head-hunters, these four were among the most dreaded as far as military skill and prowess were concerned.

The Ohaffia had neighbours with whom they had, and possibly still have, friendly or joking relations, or relations of mutual traditional enmity. Among the former were the Aro to the south of Ohaffia country as already indicated, the Ada (north), the Abam (south-west), and the Abiriba (west). Between the Ohaffia and some of these Ibo groups, for example the Ada and the Abam, traditions of common origin, rather tenuous, exist. But with the

[34] B. O. N. Eluwa, 'Ado N'idu', unpublished manuscript.

Aro the relationship was traditionally based on a common under-standing which entitled the Aro to safe passage and immunity from attack by the Ohaffia. The Aro also had the right to hire Ohaffia warriors as mercenaries to fight their wars for them. In return the Ohaffia had the freedom to raid for slaves during such wars, as well as access to Aro slave markets. At these, the Ohaffia could dispose of their captured slaves as well as of relatives who had offended by committing adultery or theft or were convicted of poisoning a close kinsman. Ohaffia mercenaries also helped the Aro to drive away troublesome or enemy neighbours.[35] The Ohaffia used these opportunities also for the hunting of human heads.

This Ohaffia–Aro friendship is termed *ukwuzì* ('asylum' or 'shelter') by the Ohaffia. The Ohaffia claim that they also took home with them, including other gifts, plenty of goats, drink, and captive women later to be married or sold.

Ukwuzì-relationships in Ohaffia can also be secured in a number of forms other than that between two different but co-operative communities, like the Ohaffia themselves and the Aro. A few examples will illustrate these forms, as well as the sacredness and the strong social recognition which an *ukwuzì*-relationship has among the Ohaffia:

(i) A man and an unmarried woman, or a widow, can enter into *ukwuzì*-relationship in which the woman (who is referred to in Ohaffia as *iko-nwânyì*) is sheltered, protected, and supported by the man, without being obliged to bring her into his house as his legal wife.[36] In this relationship the man who provides the protec-tion is entitled to the woman's favours as well as to her help on the farm. She helps to weed his farm or to carry harvested yams to the man's barn.[37]

(ii) A person can also invoke *ukwuzì*-relationship with a power-ful spirit or god. This is not in any sense the same as the *òsu*-relationship so common among the Owerri Ibo.[38] An *ukwuzì*-relationship with a powerful spirit is temporary. It lasts until the danger which the fugitive is in is over or resolved. Thus a murderer in Ohaffia could in traditional times run into a particular shrine,

---

[35] Hart, 1964, p. 27, Section 69.
[36] As in other parts of Iboland, for example, Owerri, such a woman is also called *iko-nwânyì* ('girl-friend'). In Asaba Ibo she is referred to as *m̀gbà*.
[37] See Appendix where there is a reference to this kind of relationship, p. 127.
[38] Green, 1947, pp. 12–14, 50–1, 158–9, 190–1.

such as the *Obu nkwa* in Asaga, for his safety. In this manner, he would invoke *ukwuzi*-relationship with that shrine and must not be touched. Whoever did (an unlikely imprudence), did so at his own peril. As long as the murderer remained within the precincts of the shrine, he was safe from reprisal. An *ukwuzi*-relationship can, in this same sense, be invoked by a person who is too weak to protect himself against a bully. Thus a boy who may have hurt another can run to an adult and invoke *ukwuzi* from the adult against his pursuer.

(iii) Finally, a man or a community can secure *ukwuzi*-relationship over a piece of land. Thus land, or any other form of property temporarily in one's care, protection, or use, is in such a relationship to oneself. Land pledged for a loan, or given by a weaker group to a more powerful one to be protected against encroachment from another group is in *ukwuzi*-relationship with its protector.[39]

The Abiriba had the same kind of friendly association, and still do, with the Ohaffia as did the Aro. Ohaffia tradition says that the first Abiriba immigrants (who were then known as Anauda) came from the eastern side of the Cross River as fugitives. A member of the Anauda had killed one of a neighbouring group, an act that led to the pursuit of the Anauda. The Ohaffia intervened to help the Anauda, and afterwards settled them on their present site. The Ohaffia have since remained their protectors. 'We do not hunt the heads of people who run to us for protection',[40] said an Ohaffia elder to the present writer; 'but if a head was wanted for an unexpected need in Ohaffia, any head would do, even an Ohaffia man's head.'[41] However, hunting the head of a fellow Ohaffia would be avoided.

But there also seems to be some economic and political explanations for the friendship between the Ohaffia and their Abiriba neighbours. The Abiriba Ibo have always been skilled blacksmiths and supplied the Ohaffia with most of their weapons and ammu-

---

[39] See the Appendix for an example of this kind of relationship with land.
[40] Note here the implication of *ukwuzi*-relationship in the statement.
[41] This contradiction is only apparent. Anybody who knows the Ibo would agree that it is the way they think, being always prepared in a general rule to allow that there could be exceptions. It is like saying that the impossible might even happen, e.g. 'the earth may fall upon the sky'. In practice the Ibo would defend even with his own life any person under his protection even against his own kin.

nitions of war. This served to make the Abiriba militarily indis-
pensable to the Ohaffia (as well as to other warrior groups close by)
and thus rendered them relatively immune from raids. Among the
Ibo generally blacksmiths are regarded as belonging to a sacred
guild, and as a rule must not be harmed. Thus the Awka Ibo were
also professional smiths, and similar protection was accorded them
by other Ibo groups.

To the north of Ohaffia lives the other group said to be related
to them: this group is the present-day Ada. According to tradition,
they were of Ohaffia origin, and like the Abiriba were fugitives
because of their association with the death (said to be accidental)[42]
of a youth from a related kin-group. The story is that a young
mother asked the boy to fetch her some soup-leaves from a tree.[43]
In doing so he slipped and fell to his death. The young mother
and her immediate kin-group, who were in danger of reprisal,
fled to their present home. They were originally called Potopo, it
is said, not Ada as they are today.

To the north-east, the east, and the south immediately beyond
the Aro country, live the traditional enemies of the Ohaffia. These
were mainly non-Ibo communities, especially Ibibio-speaking
groups whom the Ohaffia had persistently menaced over the years,
sometimes on the invitation of friendly neighbours, such as the Aro.

The Bende Ibo to the south-west (originally partly Ibibio)
were also the traditional enemies of the Ohaffia. As recently as
April 1962 the head of a young Bende female was cut off at a
stream. The culprit, who was eventually charged, was from the
Abam Ibo group to whom the Ohaffia, as we have seen, are related.

The other neighbours of the Ohaffia are the four well-known
'mixed' communities[44] of Ikwuni, Aria, Biakpani, and Ndi-oji, all
of whom live roughly to the north-east, east, and south of Ohaffia
country.

Ohaffia Tradition of Origin

The Ohaffia tradition of origin locates their original home at
Isieke village in Ibeku territory, which lies some fifty miles to the

[42] Homicide whether accidental or deliberate is generally inexcusable among
the Ibo. See Meek, 1937, pp. 209–10.

[43] The tree (*abùbù* in Ibo) belongs to the oil-bean family; the leaves make good
soup-vegetables.

[44] These communities are said to 'stutter' when they speak Ibo; they speak
Ibo, that is, with a peculiar accent.

south-west of Ohaffia. The Ibeku themselves, like the Ohaffia, are a major Ibo sub-group. There is never the slightest doubt expressed by either the Ohaffia or the Ibeku or by the close village-neighbours of the two communities as to the truth of this story. If one asked such close neighbours whether the Ohaffia people really came from Ibeku, 'Isieke Ibeku' would be the curt reply.

The present writer once saw a water-tap that was locked against public use quietly and surreptitiously opened by an Ibeku labourer in charge of the compound in order to give water to a thirsty Ohaffia man who had let the labourer know that he was an Ohaffia. A trifling incident perhaps, but such is the strength of the tradition of the Ibeku origin of the Ohaffia people that it does serve as an 'open sesame' to members of both communities in many difficult situations.

Traditionally no Ohaffia man would shed the blood of an Ibeku man knowingly. Informants could not recall such an incident, but if it were to happen by accident the homicide would not be avenged, as would be the case if the parties involved were strangers to each other. The customary ritual cleansing of the culprit would be demanded as if the killer were a kinsman of the victim. An Ibeku person visiting an Ohaffia home on his own or in the company of other Ohaffia citizens, would be given privileged treatment as of right. He would, for example, on many occasions, be the first to be served a calabash cup of wine, or a shot of local gin, or kola-nut, or cooked meat. Of course most guests are given privileged treatment, but the Ibeku guest usually jokingly demands to be accorded such privileges, for after all he is, he will say, 'the begetter' of the Ohaffia. This is a demand which no non-Ibeku guest can appropriately make. Again, if the visitor is an adult male and a free-born citizen of Ibeku, the rights and privileges of the closed associations (except *akpan*[45]) will be accorded him almost without question if proof of his identity is not in doubt.

The following custom also seems to support the tradition of the Ibeku origin of the Ohaffia. Among both groups pot monuments are raised to the memory of ancestors. In Ibeku the custom appears to be dying, but in Ohaffia it is still very much alive. There are differences, however: in Ohaffia pots are raised to the memory of either a male or a female ancestor, while in Ibeku it was for males only. In Ohaffia the ancestral pots are accumulated and preserved

[45] See below, pp. 60–2.

and handed down from one generation to the next for as long as
the lineage persists. In both communities reverence for the pots is
deep and strong, but apparently more so in Ohaffia now than in
Ibeku where old pots have always been destroyed as new ones
came to be installed. More will be said about this custom of
ancestral pot monuments later, but it will be necessary to add, by
way of significant contrast, that among the village communities
living between Ibeku country and Ohaffia the custom is non-
existent. The Ohaffia thus point to the custom as evidence of the
truth of their claim of 'blood' kinship with the people of their
ancestral home—the Ibeku.

Ohaffia tradition attributes their migration from Ibeku to a
fight which began between two sections of Ibeku: the Osa Ibeku
and an unnamed Ibeku village. Before the migration, the Ohaffia
were called Umu-ajiji, which is the name today of the place in
Isieke village where the Ohaffia then lived. Briefly the story is as
follows: land had been leased to Umuajiji (Ohaffia) by the Ibeku.
The Umuajiji farmed their land better and therefore had prospered
more than the Ibeku. The Umuajiji became proud, boastful, and
headstrong, while the Ibeku became envious and always on edge
with the Umuajiji. Relations steadily worsened between the Ibeku
and the Um-uajiji, so that the latter, in order to provoke the Ibeku,
would sometimes bury their matchets with the sharp edges up in
Ibeku farm-paths. Yet, ironically, the fight through which the
Ohaffia-Umuajiji people lost their original home was in fact started
by two other villages against the Ibeku. The Umuajiji became
involved when some refugees, mostly women and children from
one of the villages (Osa) which were at war with the Ibeku, ran to
the Ohaffia for safety. The Ibeku were unhappy and worried that
events had turned out the way they did, and feared that the move
to Umuajiji for safety would sooner or later precipitate a confrontation with the Ohaffia (Umuajiji). The Ibeku therefore began to
plan a surprise attack upon the Ohaffia who, although they suspected that the Ibeku would be tempted to mount such an attack
upon them, were uncertain when this might come.

One night one of the refugee women, who had been cooking a
late meal, was reaching up to get some calabash dishes which were
hanging overhead on a raffia pole, when she slipped and the dishes
crashed to the floor. At that time of night the noise sounded like a
war signal. The Ohaffia people thought the Ibeku were attacking.

Panic soon spread, followed by a stealthy departure from Umua-jiji by the Ohaffia and their Osa refugee guests. As they fled, they told anyone who asked them where they were heading in such a hurry that they were going to market.[46] But people wondered how a whole community (in Ibo, *ọhà*) could be going to market (in Ibo, *afia*) at that late time of night. Hence the term: *Ọhafia*. This, the tradition says, was how the Ohaffia got their name.[47]

The Tradition of Ohaffia Matriliny

There is one important cultural difference between the Ibeku Ibo and the Ohaffia Ibo. Whereas the Ibeku, like most other Ibo communities, have patrilineal or father-oriented social systems, today the Ohaffia have markedly matrilineal or mother-centred systems.

There are three versions of how the Ohaffia people acquired their matrilineage. One says that their refugee guests from Osa Ibeku kept themselves separate from the rest of the Ohaffia. As a group in a minority, the Osa were reluctant to part with their daughters as wives to the Ohaffia. If they did so, they accepted no marriage payment, and so were able to insist that the children of such marriages would inherit from them and would belong to their descent group. The Ohaffia, however, asked for and received marriage payments for any daughters they married to the Osa. The Ohaffia thus lost their rights over their sons' as well as their daughters' children: a poor deal as they came to realize; for what they gained in cash they lost in men, unlike their refugee guests, who multiplied more rapidly than they. This was why, according to this version of the tradition, the Ohaffia in the end adopted matriliny. This tradition, translated into historical terms, might support the view that the Ohaffia borrowed matriliny, but it is interesting that this myth represents the institution of matriliny as the result of structural relations between the two migrant groups: Umuajiji and the Osa strangers who together form the Ohaffia.

A second version of the origin of Ohaffia matriliny derives from a fuller version of the tradition of the Ohaffia migration which I have not given here. The story of their flight and journey north-eastwards refers to pregnant women who at one stage or another in the wanderings of the Ohaffia people had to be abandoned,

---

[46] Markets are held at night in parts of Iboland.

[47] As pointed out earlier, the name 'Ohaffia' is taken to be an abbreviation for a whole sentence.

either because such women were in labour and were causing delay, or because it was suspected that they would give birth to twins, which was an abomination. The women were in each case left in the charge and care of a brother or a husband, and such abandoned women, it is said, became the founders of new Ohaffia settlements. In fact, certain Ohaffia villages do have, in one form or another, traditions of female founders.[48]

The third version of the origin of matriliny again reflects the significance of the symbolic figure of the female in Ohaffia traditions. This version speaks of the flight of an Ohaffia man who had killed a fellow Ohaffia, probably a close relative, allegedly by accident. He had fled to a 'brother' (a patrilineal kinsman), who, however, returned him to his relatives. The murderer managed to escape again and on this occasion ran to a 'sister' who, rather than give her 'brother' up, chose to offer her own head in place of his. It was in this manner that the man was saved. Years later, when dying, he thought that he should show his gratitude for the self-sacrifice of his 'sister'. This he did by passing all he had in the way of worldly possessions to her children. 'For why', he said, 'should the sweat of my brow go to my own kinsmen who failed me at a time of trouble?' It was in this manner, according to this version, that Ohaffia people came to adopt matriliny. It was the man's wish, says this tradition, that all Ohaffia should do so. It is a saying in Ohaffia that a man's worst enemy is his patrikin, and his best friend his matrikin. Most Ibo have similar sayings.

There are cases of traditions in Ohaffia in which the part that women played in the founding of certain villages or lineage groups is acknowledged and even ritually rehearsed from year to year. In the village of Amuma, for example, there is an annual rite in memory of the village origin. In this a woman is the leading performer. Again, according to the tradition of origin of a certain patrilineage in the village of Amaekpu, the mother's brother's daughter of the successful male founder of the patrilineage was essential for the success of the foundation. According to this tradition, earlier attempts by other men to found a settlement had failed because 'the land was too hot for them, and nothing would grow upon it'. The successful founder[49] 'was in danger of perishing

[48] More will be said about this later.

[49] The name of the successful patrilineage is Ndi-Uyo; the language used here is figurative. 'To grow' means 'to have children or to increase and multiply'. Similarly, 'hot' means 'barren', 'infertile'. See the Appendix, p. 124.

too, as others were before him, but he took a priest's advice to bring in his mother's brother's daughter (*Ada nne*)[50] as wife to live with him so that the land might cool, and things might grow again'. There is a parallel here with similar traditions about the founding of villages in the Trobriands, where it is said that 'Each sub-clan was originated by an ancestress, frequently accompanied by her brother, who emerged from the underworld in a particular spot.'[51] We shall take up the subject of Ohaffia matriliny again later.

[50] See the Appendix, p. 111.

[51] B. Malinowski, *The Sexual Life of Savages*, London, 1929, p. 155. See also Schneider and Gough, *Matrilineal Kinship*, Berkeley and Los Angeles, Cal., 1961, p. 237.

II

FARMING, SLAVE-TRADE, AND WARFARE

Men and Women: Division of Labour

THE Ohaffia claim that in the past they lived by farming, trade, and warfare. While their traditional occupation was farming, it is likely that it was mainly the responsibility of the womenfolk, as it still is, more than of the men, who were pre-occupied with external trade and warfare. In this they resembled the other three head-hunting communities of Ada, Abam, and Abiriba. Ohaffia women are considered by other Ibo groups to be the hardest-worked on the farm of any Ibo womenfolk, just as the men are regarded as being among the hardiest travellers. And the men are often ridiculed for the hard use they put their women to. These local generalizations must, however, be accepted with reservations. In most parts of Iboland today travel is general. The old men and women farm, while the younger men and their wives go away to the townships to trade or to be employed in the Civil Service, or in the big trading firms, or in the professions.

We may speculate that Ohaffia womenfolk may have assumed their dominant role in farm-work as a result of the migration of Ohaffia people to their present territory. It is quite likely that the need for the men to consolidate a new territory or even to expand it would involve them in constant warfare and therefore in reallo-cation of responsibilities by transferring farm-work to the women. The longer this need persisted the likelier this expedient for survival would become a routine way of living. It is significant that it is largely among the central and the Cross River Ibo that farm-work has squarely been transferred to the women. In these areas the population density is high and land is scarce. Among the riverain and other Ibo who occupy the more ample and more fertile lands, farming is entirely the men's occupation.

In Ohaffia the men raise prestige crops only, particularly yams which do not usually carry the household through a one-year cycle of normal subsistence, while the women grow the real staple crops, and in addition carry the continuous work of weeding the farm over the whole agricultural year. For example, women grow maize and cassava (just as men do), and the coco-yam and beans of various kinds. They raise numerous vegetable foods, such as those we have already named.[1] These form the main family diet all year round. They gather semi-wild food-plant products, cultivate small groves of banana and plantain in their village gardens close by the household compounds, prepare and store all these either for future household use or for trade.

Apart from the cultivation of the yam, the men's share of farm-labour is limited to the planting and exploiting of oil palm, raffia (for its wine, and the leaves for thatching), coconut (owned by women as well), and kola-nut trees. There is therefore not only a sex division of farm labour, but of crops, although with some overlap. The more versatile farm tool, the hoe, is a woman's tool in Ohaffia. But this is not so in those Ibo communities where farming is squarely a man's occupation, where the hoe is clearly a man's tool and much bigger and heavier. In Ohaffia it is used by the womenfolk to weed, plant, dig, harvest, root, and even cut, with a degree of dexterity and deftness that can hardly be equalled by a man's matchet for similar activities. The Ohaffia mother can safely lodge her hoe over her shoulder without it getting in her way when suckling her baby, and carrying, as often happens, a load of cassava or coco-yam on her head at the same time. In size, weight, and shape, the tool is small, light, and like the figure 7.

A man's tools are different. He has the matchet, for example, which is some thirty inches long and four inches broad. It tends to broaden towards the tip and suddenly to taper to a point. It is thin and flat, and can best be employed for cutting, and can as easily sever the branch of a tree as it would a human head. It is in fact both a work-tool and a weapon, which a woman's hoe is not. And it is used to best advantage when standing or stooping slightly and at an arm's length from the object. It therefore perfectly suits the kind of occupation which, by tradition, Ohaffia menfolk are widely associated with, namely, cutting and cleaning of bush, harvesting palm fruits, fetching raffia poles or fronds, tapping wine, and of course head-hunting (although a much superior kind of matchet was used for this during warfare, or for ritual killing).

[1] For the botanical names of these plants, see above, pp. 6–7.

The men also have another type of tool (*ǹtùtù*), incorrectly called a 'hoe', but which is more like a spade. It has a nine-foot-long wooden handle, at one end of which is fastened a flat triangular blade, made of metal. It can best be used by men standing, or stooping a little, or kneeling, not often requiring the user to bend down from the hips as the womenfolk are obliged to do with their hoe. The 'spade' is used for making yam holes during the planting season, and for harvesting the same crop.

The Ohaffia menfolk, as I have said, are poor farmers, and contrast with such other Ibo communities as the Udi, Nsukka, and Anam whose young and able-bodied men trade their skill as migrant farm labourers for wages during the farming season. Ohaffia menfolk are never known to provide, as these do, any such labour for other Ibo communities who might need it.

Farming Cycle

Ohaffia farming cycle is best described in terms of month-by-month activities on the farm:

(i) *Late December—early January*. This is the time when the search for new bush, *ipie àlì* ('probing land' for the year's farming), begins. The adult male farmers of a given patrilineage meet to decide which matrilineages to approach for farmland. Most lands are owned by matrilineages in Ohaffia. If satisfied with the area of land offered them, their elders (*ndi ichin*) would fix a day on which the bush is to be allotted to the farmers in blocks. Farms in Ohaffia generally stretch for a mile or two.

(ii) *Late January—early February*. Bush-clearing starts soon after apportioning of farmlands. A man does it on his own or with what help he can get. At this time of year the prevailing wind is the harmattan, a dry north-easterly wind from across the Sahara. Cleared bush tends to dry up quickly, generally within *izù àtọ* (three 'weeks'), when bush-burning is done. Care is taken to avoid hasty firing of cut bush as this may result in bad burning and add unnecessarily to the work of farm clearing, which in turn may delay planting, or mean doing this in a hurry.

(iii) *Late March—April*. The making of yam mounds begins soon after farm clearing. By now the first stormy spells of rain may have occurred. Yam is the first crop to be planted by men. The period following the planting is one of anxiety for rain.

(iv) *Early May*. The planting of yam is followed by the planting

of maize. Women start sowing their vegetable crops at the beginning of May. The female head, *ezè nwanyì*, of the village womenfolk leads the sowing with a ritual hoe. She merely touches the
earth to proclaim that other women can now begin to sow. It is at
this time that okro, *añàrà*, pumpkin, melon, and the broad-leaved
vegetables are planted, when the rains come fairly steadily but
still not too heavy to harm delicate shoots. Then follow the coco-
yam[2] and the cassava in that order. These are hardier crops, not in
general danger of being damaged by the now regular and more
sustained downpours of rain. Both are also avid crops and slower in
coming to maturity. They are planted later than the yam, the king-
crop, to give the latter a good head-start. As one can see, the sowing
of crops is staggered. This is done partly with an eye to the lean
months, *unwu*.

(v) *June*. Women return to the farms in June to check on sown
crops and to repeat the sowing if some of the earlier seeds have
failed to sprout. This is called *ile akuku* ('inspecting sown seeds').

(vi) *July—August*. The first major weeding takes place in early
July, followed in late August by a second weeding, *ikpukpò ahihia*
('knocking down weeds'). Weeding is entirely women's work,
unlike certain parts of Iboland, for example, Western Ibo, where it
is strictly men's activity.

(vii) *April—July*. This is the so-called 'hunger period' (*unwu*),[3]
which stretches across both the planting months and the period
when crops are growing. At this time households fall back on
saved corn food. This has been cooked, dried, and stored from
the previous corn harvest.

(viii) *August—September*. Yam harvesting which starts in late
August or early September completes the farming cycle.[4] It is
ushered in by the first fruit rite (*Ìfèjiǫku*).

(ix) *Late October—December*. But systematic harvesting of yam
does not begin until late October when yam is dug up, cleaned,

---

[2] Not many farmers in Ohaffia are keen, as the Owerri Ibo are, on the coco-
yam. Those who grow it in Ohaffia use it largely for local trade.

[3] *Unwu* ('hunger period') is not, as generally believed, the same thin gas famine.
Famine suggests 'extreme and general scarcity of food' (*Shorter Oxford English
Dictionary*). Among the Ibo in general, *unwu* is the result of bad food distribution or over-eating and wasting of food during the harvest season when food is
plentiful and ritual feasts are given.

[4] There are at times two yam harvests during a single year. The first is of
yams planted in clay soils (*ala urǫ*); the second harvest is of yams planted on
dry land.

and temporarily reburied, waiting to be finally transferred to the barns where they are secured horizontally to poles. Household needs are met in strictly regulated quantities brought home week by week (*izù n'izù*).

November and December are also the months when traditional merriment begins, when men take new wives or give their daughters away in marriage, or perform *igbu ewu* ('killing of goats'), a rite that precedes the giving of a daughter away in marriage. It is at this period that new homes come into being.

Warfare

The part played by warfare in the Ohaffia traditional economy can be made comprehensible from two ethnographic studies: one by Horton on the Nike Ibo,[5] and by Harris on the Mbembe peoples.[6] I take Horton's study first. The Nike live in 'areas of great agricultural fertility'[7] directly to the north-west of the Ada and the Ohaffia (see Map 3). To the south of Nike and adjacent to it are the Agbaja[8] and other Ibo communities who, unlike the Nike, inhabit over-populated 'areas of exhausted, barren lands'.[9] In the past, because of poverty and the fear of hunger, the Agbaja were obliged 'to sell their kith and kin into slavery in order to obtain food'.[10] Nike served as a ready market for such slaves, 'especially as its abundant land provided the wealth to acquire them in commerce and also seize them by force with the aid of the Ada mercenaries hired by the Aro, who were the ultimate recipients of many of them'.[11]

Three factors, all vital to a prosperous trade relationship are indicated here by Horton, namely: (i) a source for the supply of food and slaves which Nike and the adjacent communities provided; (ii) the Aro traders as ready buyers of food and slaves; and (iii) a mercenary force, the Ada, used by the Nike and the Aro to

[5] W. R. G. Horton, 'The *Ohu* System of Slavery in a Northern Ibo Village-group', *Africa*, xxiv (Oct. 1954), 311–36.

[6] R. Harris, 'The Influence of Ecological Factors and External Relations on the Mbembe Tribes of South-east Nigeria', *Africa*, xxxii (Jan. 1962), 38–52.

[7] Horton, 1954, p. 312.

[8] Not the Agbaja studied by M. M. Green in *Ibo Village Affairs*, London, 1947.

[9] Horton, 1954, p. 312.   [10] Ibid., p. 311.

[11] Ibid., p. 311. That 'the Abam, Abiriba, Awhawfia [='Awhafia'] and Edda [Ada]' were used by the Aro as mercenaries was also reported by P. A. Talbot, in *The Peoples of Southern Nigeria*, London, 1926, p. 184.

acquire slaves. This tripartite trade relationship between the Nike, the Ada, and the Aro can be shown to have a geographical axis (see Map 3). At the north end of the axis was Nike country, and located at its southern end, Aro country. Between the two were the domains of the Ada and the Ohaffia (see Map 3), two related warrior communities who claimed a long-standing friendship with the Aro as well as with the Nike.[12]

The study by Harris on the Mbembe peoples sheds its own light by inference on the slave-raiding activities of the Ohaffia and on the pattern of their territorial expansion. Mbembe country lies in two ecological zones, the forest and the grassland. The forest zone, which lies directly to the north-east of Ohaffia country, has a higher rainfall which, with its forest vegetation, will mean

that streams carry more water for longer periods than they do farther north, and the consequence is that the southern valleys tend to be marshy and can be crossed only with the aid of numerous tree trunks and bamboo bridges and dug-out canoes. Movement is therefore more difficult south of the river than might be expected . . . To the visiting anthropologist the south was a land of narrow forest paths . . .; the north of shadeless country of wide views and distant hills.[13]

With this contrast in the ecology of the Mbembe country in mind, the pattern of the push by the Northern Ibo and by the Ohaffia Ibo to the south-west against the Mbembe (with the resulting turmoil) becomes intelligible. Harris notes this two-pronged pressure upon the Mbembe who 'have been pushed at least twenty miles south-eastwards by the advancing north-east Ibo'.[14] For example, 'the Osopong formerly lived wholly north of the river, but the North Eastern Ibo pushed them steadily southwards until some were forced to move over the Cross River where they came into conflict principally with the Adun . . .'[15] Similar pressures on the Mbembe came 'from non-Mbembe groups, notably Nko (Yako), Ayiga, and Igbo[16] to their west and south-west'.[17]

[12] It has already been noted that the Ohaffia claimed that this friendship existed between them and the Aro.

[13] Harris, 1962, p. 44.   [14] Ibid.   [15] Ibid.

[16] This must refer to the Ada and the Ohaffia 'Igbo' who live to the 'west and south-west' of the Mbembe; see Map 3.

[17] Reports of similar conflict are also to be found in the accounts of earlier travellers: B. J. Walker in his 'Notes of a Visit, in May 1875, to the Old Calabar and Qua Rivers, the Ekoi Country and the Qua Rapids', *Journal of the Manchester Geographical Society*, xiv (1898), 224.

Finally, Harris refers to the unwholesome activities of the Aro slave-dealers and 'Long Juju' ritual experts, actively peddling their 'oracle' and using the power of their religion over the neighbouring peoples to turn the area into a state of 'persistent fighting and turmoil'. The Aro gave 'guns and gun-powder, and slaves in exchange for quantities of dried meat and pepper and processed camwood'.[18] We learn from other sources that 'it was for the suppression of this state of things that the Aro Field Force was organized at Old Calabar (in 1900) and a short sharp campaign of three months sufficed to put an end to it. The towns belonging to the truculent natives were burned, and a wholesome lesson given to the inhabitants of the power of law and order.'[19]

The picture that emerges from Harris' Mbembe study is then as follows: (i) That the northern portion of Mbembe country is 'a shadeless country of wide open views and distant hills', but the south is broken, densely forested with marshy valleys; movement is extremely difficult without other aids. This part of the country, significantly, is adjacent to Ada and Ohaffia territories (see Map 3). (ii) That before the advent of the British rule, according to local traditions, the whole area along the Cross River was in perpetual unrest, with local groups fighting and 'jockeying for position'.[20] (iii) That Aro slave-traders and 'Long Juju' ritual experts were active in the whole area encouraging unrest by supplying guns and ammunition 'in exchange for quantities of dried meat and pepper and processed camwood'.

Ohaffia traditions of warfare and head-hunting exploits fit the above picture. These traditions speak of *ukwuzi* relationship between the Ohaffia and the Aro, similar to the 'long-standing friendship' which Horton said existed between the Aro and the Nike, and between the Ada and the Aro. Ohaffia traditions speak of the role of the Ohaffia as Aro mercenaries for which they were paid in kind: goat, drink, and access to slave markets, and certainly guns and gunpowder. The location of Ohaffia country and their head-hunting tradition would explain the references made by their non-Ibo neighbours east of the river to the 'head-hunting forays'[21] in which the Ohaffia engaged. Such forays, said Harris, made the forest 'a more dangerous place than the grassland, since surprise attack must have been so much easier where there was

---

[18] Harris, 1962, p. 45. [19] MacAlister, 1902, p. 634.
[20] Harris, 1962, p. 46. [21] Ibid., p. 47.

thick cover'.[22] She further suggests that the 'difference in the pattern of aggression, as led by 'the Ibo of the northern grasslands' and by 'the head-hunting Ibo of the south' would also explain 'the greater sparsity of non-Ibo population in the forested south . . .'. The Ohaffia and the Ada Ibo of the south to whom obviously this reference was made, took the lands of the indigenous people 'directly by force', rather than squeezing them out.[23] It seems self-evident that the Ohaffia served the Aro in the same role as the Ada did in the slave-raiding activities of the Nike and their Aro customers. It will be remembered that the Ohaffia say that they are related to the Ada.

That the Ohaffia and the Ada, as mercenaries of the Aro, raided for slaves, that the Aro themselves transported the slaves not only from the Cross River area but from as far afield as Igala in Northern Nigeria, using the highland route of which mention has already been made, can in some measure be historically confirmed. The record of remembered experiences of liberated slaves who were taken from the eastern parts of Iboland and beyond would appear to provide this measure of confirmation. The slaves were interviewed in Freetown, Sierra Leone, in 1853, by the Revd. S. W. Koelle.[24] What they remembered and said about their home, age, married status before they were captured and subsequently sold into slavery, about the manner of their capture, and the crimes for which they were sold, would be of some interest. The evidence supports the view already given here about the role and the activities of the Nike, the Ada, the Ohaffia, and the Aro, in and around the Cross River country, and in parts of Iboland; also about the slave routes used. Some of the statements made by the slaves are briefly reported below.

George Wilhelm of Freetown, whose real name was 'Akowilo' (Akuwilo is a well-known Ibo name which means 'wealth is envy'), remembered that he was sold into slavery by his own relatives. He was born, he said, 'in the town of Umozuo [Umuasua] in Isoama [Isu Ama in Central Ibo] west of Oru [in Orlu Division]'. He said that 'Isoama' was west of 'Nkalo'. There is Nkalu in Orlu Division although two others at least are in Uyo Division, south of Bende. The point to note here is not only that George was Ibo, or that his case was the familiar one, namely, an Ibo criminal sold into slavery

[22] Harris, 1962, p. 47.   [23] Ibid., p. 43.
[24] The Revd. S. W. Koelle, *Polyglotta Africana*, London, 1854, pp. 7–8.

by his own kith and kin possibly to the Aro, but that he came from an area which was within the sphere of Aro-Ohaffia activities, not far from the Cross River, the area of turmoil.

Jacob Egypt, whose native name was Esikanyi (Ibo: *Esi nke anyi*, 'if anyone passes our way'),[25] provides an example of a liberated slave who recalled that he was 'brought to the sea' in a journey that lasted days from Igala in the north, through Ukehe in Nsukka, clearly down the highland route already mentioned, to Aro and from there to the sea.[26]

Thomas O'Connor, whose true name was Aneke ('land is not divided'), was sold into slavery by a treacherous friend, and brought from Igala (like Jacob Egypt above) 'in succession to Aro, Bendo [Bende], and Obane [Bonny, a slave port]'.

George Rose (his Ibo name was Adibe, meaning 'there is no rival') recalled that he was 'born in Isoama [Isu Ama] country whence he was stolen when a little boy . . . brought up in the village of Asaga [in Aro country, not I think the Ohaffia Asaga] was sold to the Portuguese in Obane [Bonny] at about the age of twenty-four years'. He spoke Aro Ibo dialect, and recalled the names of such places as Ihe, south of Ohaffia, and Itu, south of Aro, and 'Kalaba' (Calabar), as well as 'Ibibia' (Ibibio). He remembered too how long his journeys took to 'Kalaba'. 'There is no native of Aro in Sierra Leone', he said. This confirms the notion that the Aro probably were loth to sell fellow Aro into slavery.

John Thomas, whose true name was Okon [an Efik/Ibibio name], was from 'Mbofia' [there are several 'Obuohia', including one north of Bende, although his 'Mbofia', he said, was 'east of Benda [Bende]'. John Thomas recalled that he was sold on account of adultery and brought to Bonny. He also remembered the name of the river, 'Enyim' [the Cross River];[27] he made mention of Ututu (in Ihe), 'Ebireba' (Abiriba), and 'Benda' (Bende).

All in all, these testimonies, though they were not all from Ibo slaves, seem to support the view suggested here that the Aro, with the aid of their mercenaries, were active in and around the middle Cross River area, capturing and transporting slaves down to the

[25] This veiled threat or boast is a recognized Ibo name.
[26] The mention of Igala, a Northern Nigeria people around the junction of the Niger and the Benue rivers, suggests that Jacob Egypt (Esikanyi) must have been sold and resold.
[27] This Efik river-name is also the name (though in corrupt form) of the Ohaffia stream Inyam. See Map 2.

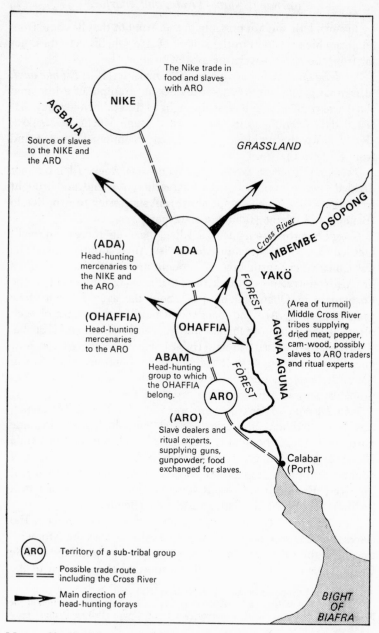

The Nike trade in food and slaves with ARO

AGBAJA

Source of slaves to the NIKE and the ARO

NIKE

GRASSLAND

Cross River

MBEMBE OSOPONG

ADA

(ADA)
Head-hunting mercenaries to the NIKE and the ARO

YAKÖ

FOREST

(OHAFFIA)
Head-hunting mercenaries to the ARO

OHAFFIA

(Area of turmoil)
Middle Cross River tribes supplying dried meat, pepper, cam-wood, possibly slaves to ARO traders and ritual experts

ABAM
Head-hunting group to which the OHAFFIA belong.

FOREST

AGWA AGUNA

ARO

(ARO)
Slave dealers and ritual experts, supplying guns, gunpowder; food exchanged for slaves.

Calabar (Port)

(ARO) Territory of a sub-tribal group

Possible trade route including the Cross River

Main direction of head-hunting forays

BIGHT OF BIAFRA

MAP 3. Sketch Map showing Sphere of Slave Trade and linking the Nike, the Ada, the Ohaffia, and the Aro, in the Cross River Area.

sea via Calabar to Bonny where the Portuguese and other European dealers were waiting to receive them. The testimonies also lend credence to the view that the highland route did serve as a slave route.

The slave-trade thus encouraged hostility in the Cross River area. The opportunity which the world trade in slaves provided was ruthlessly exploited by the Aro with the aid of the three very warlike Ibo communities, the Ada, the Abam, and the Ohaffia. The topography of the area, the north-to-south trends of the Okigwi-Udi-Aro ridge and the Cross River, facilitated movement and access from the north, possibly ultimately linking the trans-Saharan routes, to the Atlantic in the south (see Map 3).

It is interesting also to note in this connection the peculiar Ohaffia greeting to a visitor. In welcoming one, they do not say, as most other Ibo communities would, *nno* ('welcome'), or *I biala?* ('have you come?'). Instead, they ask, *Udo dìkwà?* ('peace, is it there?'). Nor do the Ohaffia offer the visitor the traditional kola first, as do most Ibo. Rather, they first offer a wooden bowl (*okwa*) containing a ball of white chalk (*nzu*) which signifies *obì ọcha* ('whiteness of heart' or 'good intentions') among the Ibo. The visitor is expected, or even urged, to touch the white ball of chalk and rub it on the back of his hand. Then kola is offered, or, if already in the bowl, is split and shared. This manner of greeting is perhaps comprehensible only in terms of the strong tradition of warfare which the Ohaffia have had.

Today the Ohaffia have abandoned warfare and head-hunting. But the role of these activities during the slave-trade can be seen to have been important in the external relations of the tribal groups who inhabit this old Cross River trade corridor.

Trade and Travel

Firm evidence that the Ohaffia gained much material wealth from their trade association with the Aro in the past is lacking. The Ohaffia claim that they collected fees in the form of booty—food and slaves mainly. But none of the foreign treasures which could be acquired through such trade association and exchange, and which would serve as evidence, survive today in Ohaffia. There are no John Bull jugs, colourful Spanish enamel plates, big multi-coloured chiefly umbrellas, king and queen manillas, and Victorian antiques (copper kettles and lamps, or ship captain's cork helmets, bush shirts, sheathed swords, cannons, and the like), such as can still be found today in the houses of the Efik of Calabar, and mixed Ibo, Ijaw, Kalabari, and Okrika communities of the Bonny, Opobo, and Okrika towns.

It is difficult to escape the impression that the Aro came off better than the Ohaffia in this trade association, as one might perhaps expect. MacAlister remarked: 'During the rebuilding of the [Aro] towns which were burned during the war many [copper] rods were unearthed.'[28] He further noted that 'many of the chiefs had amassed great wealth at Bendi—the most northerly town in the field of operations. A case was discovered in the bush containing hundreds of pounds' worth of copper rods, together with guns and other weapons, war drums, tom-toms, and so on.'[29]

In Aro Chuku today one can still find impressive evidence of the ancient wealth accumulated through trade as middlemen and ritual experts. In Ohaffia this is not so, nor are slave groups found in the same strength as they are in Aro Chuku or Nike country. Even today relatively few Ohaffia people have made fortunes in petty trade as their Abiriba neighbours have, although several hundreds of them, like the latter, engage in it in Efik and Ibibio towns like Calabar, Oron, Ikot-Ekpene, and Uyo, and many more in Ibo townships like Aba, Umuahia, and Port Harcourt. There they peddle yams, stockfish, local heavy twines, tobacco, smuggled Spanish gin, and imported cotton prints retailed in cut lengths ready, more or less, to wear.

The Ohaffia still travel, although now no more than other Ibo do, especially the Ibo of Owerri and Onitsha provinces where land is scarce and population heavy. The Ohaffia accepted education rather earlier than most Ibo. This may explain why their main attraction is to the Civil Service where several of them serve as clerks, police, and soldiers. Teaching in mission schools is also popular. They are among the ablest in the field of education in Nigeria. This is clearly the result of missionary activities pioneered in Ohaffia by the Revd. Robert Collins of the Free Scotland Mission, who worked for about a quarter of a century (1911–33), converting the people to the Christian faith through education.

[28] MacAlister, 1902, p. 632.   [29] Ibid.

III

GROUPS AND LOCALITY IN OHAFFIA

The Problem of Terminology

IN a sense, the problem is one of vagueness on the part of the Ibo in their use of kinship and local terms when referring to local units of varying scale in their social organization. In explaining this further, I can do no better than to refer to the views of two writers.

Ardener, for example, in reference to Ibo system of kinship, points out that only two terms, *ǝmǝ nnɛ* and *ǝmǝ nna*, 'have to meet the needs of a whole lineage system'.[1] The result is that these terms are, as it were, over-stretched in their use: thus they can only be comprehensible within the context of their application. The same element of vagueness is also present in the use of local terms. On this, Ardener writes: 'In using such local terms as *obodo, ala, nga, ebeke, mba*, an Ibo may have in mind any size of group from the smallest cluster of compounds to the largest aggregate possible. Indeed, all can be translated "country" and serve to describe Nigeria itself.'[2] He concludes that 'this vagueness of application of local terms means that any attempt to assign them to groups of a definite size, and especially to arrange them in any hierarchy of increasing magnitude, is doomed to failure.'[3]

Miss Green, an earlier writer on the Ibo, and on the same problem, was just as blunt: 'In every case it is the context which gives precision to the term and we deceive ourselves if we think that the terms like these can be defined apart from their context.'[4]

Terminological difficulties of the sort indicated will be met with here. Such local terms as 'village-group', 'village', and the like, may have to be used to describe the Ohaffia pattern of social organization. My 'solution' is to make an arbitrary choice from

---

[1] Ardener, 'Lineage and Locality among the Mba-Ise Ibo', *Africa*, xxix (1959), 117–19. The problem could not be more neatly set out than in the pages referred to here.
[2] Ibid. [3] Ardener, 1959, p. 117.
[4] Green, 1947, p. 17. The terms she refers to here are *ǝnama, imɛ obi.*

terms already devised by other anthropologists, but first I note their criteria and then look at my own material before making the choice, but it is a choice which, I admit, may not always be ideal.

The Ohaffia as a Corporate Group

An official report on the Ohaffia in the 1930s notes that the people have always been 'conscious that they are a corporate body'.[5] The Ohaffia themselves say that the basis of their strong feeling of corporateness lies in their past history. They make the claim in their oral tradition that in the past their villages met, as they still do, when there was need to take decisions on matters that affected their general interest and which also called for urgent and concerted action. Drought, epidemic, external threat, or even the presence of man-eating or crop-destroying beasts were causes to make them meet as a community.

I give one illustrative example which concerns the danger from crop-destroying beasts. The Ndi Edike lineage unit of Amafia[6] is regarded by many other Ohaffia groups as being able to transform their male members into bush-hogs. As a result they are believed to have the power of protecting their own crops and the crops of related or friendly groups against the destructive activities of genuine bush-hogs. They play a prominent part in the Ohaffia New Yam Festival (*Ifejioku*) which takes place in Amaekpu annually in late August or early September.

The Ohaffia, as a community, own a common tutelary spirit, *Ikwan*, a war spirit, whose shrine with that of his wife, *Orie*,[7] is at Elu where the first migrant group settled after their 'quick' departure from Isieke Ibeku. From Elu some of the migrants later scattered in different directions to found satellite settlements. This ancestral shrine is in a sacred grove called *ukwu mgbo*, and consists mainly of raffia palm. It is on an elevated site close to the first mission house in Ohaffia.

The Ohaeke Villages

What appears at first sight to be the evidence of 'dual organization' in the grouping of Ohaffia local units involves certain villages,

---

[5] J. C. Mayne, op. cit.

[6] Amafia is a primary division of Amaekpu village. See below.

[7] It is worth noting that on Orie weekday no one in the whole of Ohaffia should go to farm or undertake any activity that could be construed as farmwork.

eight in number, which call themselves the *Ohaeke*.[8] These villages
each have the special right to run a powerful political and administrative body of their own, called *Umuaka*.[9] This right is denied
the remaining seventeen villages which, however, do not recognize
themselves as a group, nor act as one in opposition to the Ohaeke
villages. On the contrary, they tend to accept as a matter of course
the superior status of the Ohaeke villages. More will be said about
Umuaka later. The free-born members of each of the eight Ohaeke
villages refer to themselves as the *amadi* ('notables' or 'true sons')
of Ohaffia. It is interesting to note that although all but one of the
twenty-five Ohaffia villages claim common descent, it is only these
eight who enjoy the right to Umuaka in their various villages. A
possible explanation is that the Ohaffia villages not represented
were daughter villages. It is likely, however, that they were not all
derived from the eight, but that some of them were attracted to
settle by the power of the eight and in the Ibo manner are now
regarded as Ohaffia. This puzzle cannot be unravelled as no explanation was sought in the field. It is interesting too that five of
the eight Ohaeke villages are to the west of the ridge, and the
remaining three on the ridge itself, while the vast majority of the
satellite villages lie east of the ridge. This appears to confirm
the view that the direction of later Ohaffia expansion was eastwards
towards the Cross River, with the older settlements to the west.

Recent 'Functional' Units

Next in scale to the division, vaguely 'dual', of the Ohaffia into
the Ohaeke and 'non-Ohaeke' villages, is the recent grouping of
the Ohaffia as a whole into four main local units, namely, Isiama,
Ania, Okamu, and Ohafor. This grouping occurred in the 1940s
primarily for the purposes of self-help. A few years later, in the
early 1950s, the units were officially constituted into four local
council areas for the modern political purposes of local and regional

---

[8] The Ohaeke villages are Elu, Amaekpu, Ebem (all three are on the ridge),
Okagwe, Ndi Anku, Oboro, Ndi Uduma Ukwu, and Nkwoebi (all five are to the
west of the ridge). The etymology of the name Ohaeke is in part obscure. The
element, *oha*, we already know to mean 'people'. *Eke*, depending on the tone,
is either the name of an Ibo weekday (*Èke*) or that of a snake, *Eke* ('python').
Ohaeke, therefore, may mean 'people who meet on the Eke market-day', or
'people of the python', with the implication of sacredness or power.

[9] There are ambiguities in the etymology of the word, *umuaka*. Tonally,
umùaka in Ibo means 'children'. But the element, *Akà*, as a proper name means
'precious' or 'dear', being also the name of a bead.

elections. Later we shall show that the division was arbitrary, that its basis was territorial rather than of descent, and that the general tendency to regroup along functional lines is very typical of the Ibo.

The social objectives which the four divisions have set themselves from time to time both as co-operative and competing units before their present role as electoral areas emerged, will be discussed first. The four would co-operate to launch certain social welfare projects which the villages in any one of the units would be unable on its own to carry out, given the limited resources it must have. The idea behind the pursuit of these projects is to bring *oga n'ihu* ('going front' or 'progress') to Ohaffia.

In Ohaffia, as among the so-called general Ibo, progress is conceived of in very concrete terms and usually would take the form of a new health centre, a new maternity home, a 'national' college,[10] a new local postal agency, or pipe-borne water (locally called 'pump'). Indeed, at one time or another, the Ohaffia have successfully met these needs without initial financial aid from the Regional Government. But the Government is generally given due notice about the wish of the community to establish such needs themselves. Government gives its advice and approval if it is satisfied that such progressive schemes have met the provisions of regional planning.

Any such improvements would, as a rule, be sited in any part of Ohaffia acceptable to the four units as most suitable, the general understanding being that as soon as more resources become available the new improvement would be extended to selected villages in other units. Generally, an amenity on the scale of a 'national' college is costly to launch and to maintain, and may not count as one of those to be extended.

There is rivalry among the different adult age-sets to initiate major projects in Ohaffia. Thus any age-set which would want to be regarded as forward-looking, active body of Ohaffia citizens may decide to initiate the building of a college, or whatever else it would consider to be progressive for Ohaffia. The move by one age-set to do this is seen as a challenge to other age-sets, which

[10] It is a general practice of Ibo Improvement Unions to build schools, colleges, and even churches for their communities. The word 'national' is often tagged on to these institutions to reflect the common community feeling that produced the achievement. The Ohaffia college is properly called the Ohaffia High School.

then would try to match the challenge by initiating another new scheme.

Now having decided on what scheme to tackle, members of the age-set launching it would meet, usually at Christmas time, when most of them who work or trade outside Ohaffia can come home. The funds needed, or at least part of a set target, would be raised at the meeting. Sooner or later, government advice or approval is sought, tenders are advertised, and contracts awarded. Considerable expense is often saved by the use of communal labour which villages of each of the four big units provide in turns.

There is plenty of evidence of the co-operative activities of the Ohaffia as a community in recent times. In 1949 the Ohaffia as a whole were able to raise sufficient funds to send three of their sons to universities in the United States of America. Concerted actions of this sort have become commonplace among the Ibo, and are now taken for granted. But at that time they were unusual feats for any Ibo community of the size of Ohaffia to undertake. In subsequent years, during the late 1950s and the early 1960s, the Ohaffia were able to provide themselves with a health centre, a high school, and pipe-borne water.

Sometimes the larger and more powerful villages, particularly where they are located close together in one unit, influenced decisions on the siting of amenities. As a result, the villages in each of the four units tend now to consolidate around their largest villages to be able to counterbalance this dominating tendency.

I want now to consider the theoretical interest which this recent fourfold division of Ohaffia has for students of Ibo ethnography. The division does not seem to have any genealogical basis and can indeed be said to be arbitrary. That it is not genealogically based can be seen, in part, of course, from the presence of communities acknowledged to be of non-Ohaffia origin in some of the four units. For instance, Ihenta village in Isiama unit, and some unnamed sections in the village of Amuma in Okamu unit, are such 'foreign' groups in Ohaffia. More obviously, the etymology of the names of the four units also shows that the villages in each were grouped together on the basis of territorial proximity rather than on that of genealogy. It can of course be argued that on this basis other patterns of grouping are possible, and therefore that it is not unlikely that genealogy originally was a factor in the present grouping. This could be true, but I have no evidence that this was so.

(i) *Isiamà*, the name of one of the units,[11] consists of two elements: *isi* (meaning 'head' or 'beginning'), and *ama* ('path'). Applied to the eleven villages which make up the unit, the name means 'villages that are located at the head or at the beginning of paths'. 'Isiama' also carries the veiled implication that the eleven villages so named are the most 'enlightened' villages in Ohaffia. There is justification for the implication. For example, the Free Church of Scotland Mission, the first to bring the benefits of education and of the Christian faith to Ohaffia, has its mission house at Elu in Isiama. The post-office, the local court, as well as the local reservoir are all in Elu. The Ohaffia High School is in Ebem village in the same Isiama unit. These visible signs of progress in Ohaffia were located in this unit partly because the villages where they are sited lie on the ridge and are easily accessible from most directions. This can be seen from Map 2. It is also because the greater proportion of Ohaffia population is in this unit.

(ii) *Ànià*, the name of the second unit located to the south of Isiama, is compounded from the first letters in the names of the five villages which make up the unit. Recurring letters were dropped. Thus, 'A' is for Akanu, the largest village in the unit, as well as in Ohaffia; 'N' for the village of Ndi Uduma Awoke; 'I' for the village of Isi Ugwu; finally, 'A' for the villages of Abia and Amankwu.

(iii) *Òkàmu*, the third unit to the north-east of Isiama, was derived in the same way as Ania. The letters 'O' and 'K' stand for the village of Okoni, the largest in the unit. The next two letters, 'A' and 'M', stand for the village of Ama Ngwu, and 'M' and 'U' for Amuma. The letter 'M' has recurred in 'OK-AM-MU' and therefore one was dropped.

(iv) *Òhafòr*,[12] the name of the fourth unit to the west of Isiama, and south of Okamu, unlike the three units so far considered, was taken from the name of the market day, *Àfò*, which Asaga, the biggest village in the unit observes. The other element, *òhà*, in the name, has already been seen to mean 'people'. Therefore *Òhafòr*, as applied to the villages in the unit, would mean 'people (or villages) who attend the same *àfò* market'.

Thus the etymology of the names of the four units confirms

---

[11] See Map 2.
[12] Strictly *Òha àfò*. The text spellings are those chosen by the local people.

their territorial nature. The division provides good evidence to support Jones's view that among the Ibo such alliances are quite common and that their basis is not always descent but often territory.[13] Jones explains that this arbitrary manner in which an Ibo community divides itself into units 'of approximately equal size and weight' has its roots in 'the difficulty with a structure based on a system of descent groups . . .'. Such groups 'develop unevenly and . . . almost invariably tend to split into unduly large number of smaller segments, so that original balance is lost'.[14] Thus the structural realignment which takes place, as in the Ohaffia example, is intended to restore the equilibrium which the natural processes of descent-fission cannot be depended upon to achieve.

The fourfold division of Ohaffia villages serves the political objective of balancing out in a rough and ready manner the respective strengths of the larger villages which form the cores of the units.[15] As I have already shown, the balancing derives entirely from self-interest. And as Jones points out, 'such adjustments do not of course involve any transfer of territory or change of domicile. They merely mean that the transferred group faces a new central meeting-place and shares and works in the segment to which it has been transferred.'[16]

Settlement Pattern in Ohaffia—Villages

I have been discussing the four principal units into which the Ohaffia have recently grouped themselves. I have also shown that it was primarily for the purposes of self-help. The basis of the grouping, as we have seen, is not obviously genealogical, and it cuts across the Ohaeke-grouping. An important point that has emerged, which needs to be stressed, is the strength of common feeling among the Ohaffia as a single community.

I now proceed to discuss the general pattern which Ohaffia

---

[13] G. I. Jones, 'Dual Organization in Ibo Social Structure', *Africa*, xlx (1949), 152.
[14] Ibid.
[15] Cf. Green, 1941, p. 140, where she notes the same process of adjustment. I quote: 'It had happened with the passage of time that Umueke-owere had greatly outgrown Umueke-ama in numbers. It had, therefore, been decided to take the large extended family of Umu Nwa Ebodim out of Umueke-owere and include it in Umueke-ama so that numbers should balance in the doing of communal work.' See Jones, 1949, p. 153.
[16] Ibid.

settlements take. It is at this point that the problem of terminology arises once again.[17] Until now I have been referring to the twenty-five Ohaffia settlements as 'villages' without feeling obliged to explain why the term has been preferred to the term 'village-group'. The settlements whose structural pattern on the ground and in kinship-depth we shall be examining in some detail here are Elu, Amaekpu, and Ebem. I have, in a sense arbitrarily, called them villages. Using the criteria developed partly by Green and partly by Ardener, there are certain obstacles to calling them village-groups. The term 'village-group' is usually applied to territorial groups of greatly different genealogical and functional status. In each of the three Ohaffia settlements to be examined (for example Elu) the primary and the secondary divisions lack that degree of separation and of economic and ritual specialization which marks their equivalents in a 'typical' Ibo village-group.

Some other criteria do apply in the three Ohaffia settlements which I have called villages, in the same way as they do to those which Green and Ardener called 'village-groups'. These criteria are: the possession of a common name; location on a clearly defined territory; the sharing of 'a common market and a number of other social and economic institutions for which they accept responsibility . . .';[18] and finally, recognition of a common tutelary spirit (although each subsidiary segment may have one or more of its own). Each of my three villages has also three main levels of segmentation, which I refer to as the primary, the secondary, and the tertiary divisions, as I shall show below.

(i) *Elu* (meaning 'up' or 'on the hill') is, as we have earlier noted, sited on the ridge. The village is generally recognized by all Ohaffia as their most senior village, being as we have already stated, the site where the first Ohaffia immigrants traditionally settled. Elu has two *primary* divisions: Ekelogo and Amaihe (see Fig. 1*a*). Ekelogo, as a name, is descriptive (*eke lu ogo*: 'on a high place'), and derives from the location of the group on the upper part of the ridge relative to Amaihe. It is the senior of the two wards. Amaihe too, as a name, is descriptive (*ama ihè*: 'path to farm'). This

---

[17] Individual settlements, large or small, are referred to officially as villages; the village primary units are called *wards*, and the secondary ones *compounds*. In the chapter on Inheritance, I have retained the official terms for clarity when citing official documents but at the same time have given their equivalents as used in the discussion in this chapter.

[18] Ardener, 1959, p. 116.

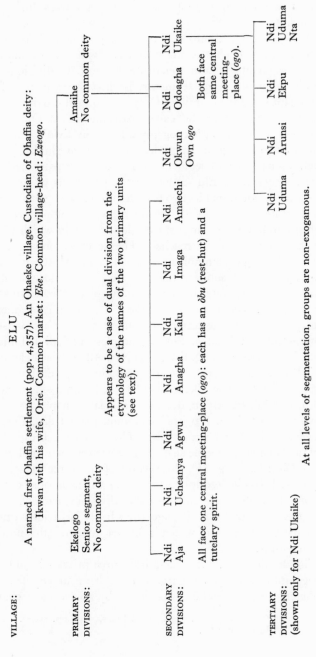

FIG. 1a. *Structure of Elu*

ELU

VILLAGE: A named first Ohaffia settlement (pop. 4,357). An Ohaeke village. Custodian of Ohaffia deity: Ikwan with his wife, Orie. Common market: *Eke*. Common village-head: *Ezeogo*.

PRIMARY DIVISIONS:

Ekelogo
Senior segment,
No common deity

Amaihe
No common deity

Appears to be a case of dual division from the etymology of the names of the two primary units (see text).

SECONDARY DIVISIONS:

Ndi Aja   Ndi Ucheanya   Ndi Agwu   Ndi Anagha   Ndi Kalu   Ndi Imaga   Ndi Amaechi

All face one central meeting-place (*ogo*): each has an *òbu* (rest-hut) and a tutelary spirit.

Ndi Okwun
Own *ogo*

Ndi Odoagha

Ndi Ukaike

Both face same central meeting-place (*ogo*).

TERTIARY DIVISIONS:
(shown only for Ndi Ukaike)

Ndi Uduma

Ndi Arunsi   Ndi Ekpu   Ndi Uduma Nta

At all levels of segmentation, groups are non-exogamous.

division is exactly of the sort which is referred to as dual by some authors.[19]

Ekelogo is divided into seven *secondary* units, and Amaihe into three (Fig. 1a). Each secondary unit is divided into a number of lineage segments. These constitute the tertiary divisions. They are the minimal lineage segments. Each such segment is further divided into extended families. Only the minimal and the secondary divisions can properly be called patrilineages in Ohaffia, even though at neither level is exogamy a factor in dividing the groups into strict genealogical categories as it does at similar and even much higher levels of segmentation among the 'patrilineal' Ibo.

The structure of Elu village on the ground is as follows: we have already noted that its two primary units, Ekelogo and Amaihe, are separated in space with the former on the upper part of the high ground, and the latter on the lower part in which direction the farmlands could be reached. The seven secondary units of Ekelogo face one common meeting-place (*ogo*). But in Amaihe, two of its three secondary units, namely Ndi Odoagha and Ndi Ukaike, face a separate common meeting-place. The third secondary unit, Ndi Okwun, has its own *ogo*. The minimal segments, as already stated, are the tertiary units. All of these are non-exogamous groups in Ohaffia. Some examples are Ndi Uduma, Ndi Arunsi, Ndi Ekpu, and Ndi Uduma Nta. All of these belong to the Ndi Ukaike secondary division (see Fig. 1a). Each secondary division, like the Ndi Ukaike, is identified with a single meeting-hut or rest-hut called *òbu*, described in a later chapter.[20]

Now, as a village, Elu has a common market-day, *Eke*, and a tutelary spirit, *Ikwan*, with his wife *Orie*. We have already learned that the Ohaffia as a whole also accept *Ikwan* as their tutelary spirit.

(ii) *Ebem* (see Fig. 1b), the second of the three villages being considered, has a descriptive name too which means 'my home' (*ebe m*). The village has three primary divisions, namely, Mgbaga, Ekelogo, and Ezukwu. Ekelogo (in Ebem) is divided into nine secondary units, each of which is further divided into a number of tertiary units.

The division of Ebem village into three primaries, and of Elu village into two, does suggest that at least in Ohaffia, to use Ardener's words, 'dual organization is by no means as character-

---

[19] Green, 1947, pp. 139–45, and Jones, 1949, pp. 150–6.
[20] In Chapter IX.

istic as it appears to be in some [other Ibo] areas, and [that] functional divisions into threes and fours are quite common.' Indeed, Amaekpu, the third village in the examples we are considering, is divided into four primaries.

FIG. 1*b*. *Structure of Ebem*

VILLAGE: EBEM

A named settlement (pop. 11,114). An Ohaeke village.
Founder: Ancestress, *Chiasara*. Common market: *Nkwo*.
Common village-head: *Ezeogo*. No common deity.

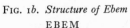

PRIMARY
DIVISION: Mgbaga   Ekelogo   Ezukwu

All share one central meeting-place (*ogo*).

SECONDARY
DIVISION:

Ndi Uzubi	Ndi Agwu	Ndi Ukpola	Ndi Ensi	Ndi Ekweke	Ndi Ukpo	Ndi Okwara	Ndi Ado	Ndi Nchara

Each of these has an *òbu* (rest-hut), and a tutelary spirit.

TERTIARY
DIVISION: No data for Ebem (see Elu, Fig. 1*a*).

At all levels of segmentation, groups are non-exogamous.

The three primary divisions in Ebem village have each their own tutelary spirits housed in the *òbu* of the senior secondary division. In Mgbaga primary division, Ndi Idika secondary unit is in charge of the tutelary spirit.[21] Ndi Uzubi secondary unit is in charge of the tutelary spirit of Ekelogo primary division, and Ndi Inyima secondary unit is in charge of that of Ezukwu primary division. The absence of a common deity in Ebem village may be explained by the fact that the village had a female founder.[22] But Ebem observes a common market-day, *Nkwo*, and its units share a number of social activities described later in common. Unlike Elu village, the three primary divisions of Ebem all face a large irregularly circular central meeting-place, *ogo*, although Mgbaga primary division does not abut directly on it. There are other paths, *ezi*, to be found, around which huts are grouped.

(iii) *Amaèkpù*, the third of the three examples of villages being discussed, is said to mean 'path' (*ama*) of a shrine called *Èkpù*. But *ekpu* is sometimes interpreted as meaning 'stooping to pass through', as one would do through a thicket. Amaekpu village is

[21] The *òbu* or the rest-hut of Ndi Idika secondary unit is described in Chapter IX.
[22] See Chapter X. Among the Ibo, women are not generally associated with important lineage shrines as custodians or founders.

divided into four primary units which are more widely separated than those of Elu or Ebem villages. We have already learned that Amaekpu provides another instance of a division other than dual.

FIG. 1c. *Structure of Amaekpu*

VILLAGE: AMAEKPU

A named settlement (pop. 9,398). An Ohaeke village. Common deity (*Ekpu*), Common *Ezeogo*, Common market, *Afǫ̀*, Common war-drum.

PRIMARY
DIVISION: Amafia   Ngodo   Ahawa   Amaoba
Senior
segment by
priority of
settlement.
Custodian of
common deity.

Amafia is where all Amaekpu can meet, but each primary division has its own meeting-place, *ogo*.

SECONDARY DIVISION:	Ndi Ofali (1)	Ndi Umuozio (2)	Ndi Edike (3)	Ndi Okewu (4)	Ndi Uche (5)	Ndi Ikuku (6)	Ndi Aja (7)	Ndi Inyima (8)

All share one central meeting-place (*ogo*). Each has its own *obu* (rest-hut), and own tutelary spirit. See Fig. 2 for those of Amafia.

TERTIARY
DIVISION: Ndi Uyo   Ndi Ukwa   ? (Incomplete data)

At all levels of segmentation, groups are non-exogamous.

Except for the greater distances, not more than a few hundred yards but sometimes less, between the four primary units, the structure of the village in lineage terms is similar in every respect to those of Elu and Ebem already described. Each primary unit in Amaekpu has its own meeting-place, *ogo*, in the heart of the unit. Amafia, a primary unit, is recognized as the senior in Amaekpu.[23] Important village meetings are held in its central meeting-place. The ground structure of Amafia is described in full below. Like the other two villages, Amaekpu had its own market day, *Afǫ*, but its four primary units have their own tutelary spirits, although they also accept Ekpu as the village deity. This is in Amafia. The tutelary spirit of the Ofali secondary unit in Amafia primary unit is regarded as the most powerful.

[23] Despite the appearance of the common Ibo term *ama* ('path') in these place-names, the Ohaffia use the term *ezi* (in general Ibo, 'compound') in their modern dialect.

The three villages we have been discussing can be described by the same structural model which consists essentially of three levels of territorial segmentation. Thus each of the villages is first divided into primary units, then the primaries are divided into secondary units which in turn are divided into tertiaries. It is significant that seven of the nine primary units which make up the three villages have descriptive names rather than personal ones. The remaining two, although their etymology is obscure, are certainly not personal names.[24] However, the smaller units, from the secondary downwards, have *ndi* names (*ndi* means 'children of' or 'people of' a named ancestor). This difference in the way in which the larger Ibo groups and the smaller ones are named supports Ardener's theory that among the Ibo 'in larger groups it is difficult to tell how for the functional divisions truly represent original lineage segments'. It also supports his surmise, stated to be based upon present-day analogy, 'that lineages and their segments which have descriptive names ("Iroko Path", etc.), rather than $\theta m\theta$-names ("Children of"), are the most likely to represent original groupings by propinquity and function'.[25] The grouping of the Ohaffia, first into four main divisions, and next into primaries, and practically all of them with descriptive names, seems to provide (at these two largest levels) support for this view.

Village Activities in Relation to Ohaffia and its Four Divisions

I now want to discuss certain village activities first before going on to consider the residential structure of the Ohaffia village primary division of Amafia in Amaekpu. My aim is to show that villages both co-operate and compete among themselves in certain areas of social and economic life. Inter-village rivalry generally is never so severe as to endanger the essential unity of the villages in any one main unit. The kind of objectives which villages may set themselves are largely economic and social.

Economic objectives. The statement by Miss Green that among the Agbaja Ibo, 'trade is second only to agriculture as a means of livelihood and is one of their ruling passions',[26] holds for the Ohaffia as it does for many other Ibo communities. One of the most obvious areas of co-operation among the villages in Ohaffia is the

---

[24] The two, Mgbaga in Ebem village, and Ahawa in Amaekpu village, are not personal names.

[25] Ardener, 1959, p. 131.

[26] Green, 1947, p. 12.

market-place. Like the rest of the Ibo, they have four days to the week, all of which are market days.

Where the villages are numerous, severe limitation on trade is imposed by the four-day week, as there will not be enough market days to go round, especially if the villages are located close together,[27] as indeed they are in Ohaffia. To overcome this difficulty the Ohaffia have made their four-day week into an eight-day one simply by duplicating each of the four market-days, so that *Èke*, *Oriè*, *Àfọ̀*, and *Nkwọ* (the Ibo names of the days) each occur twice. By referring to one *Eke*, for instance, as *Eke ukwu* (*Eke* 'big'), and the other as *Eke nta* (*Eke* 'small'), and making the same distinction with *Orie*, *Afọ*, and *Nkwọ*, the confusion from duplication which might otherwise arise is avoided.

The four big market-days were then assigned to the four main units of Ohaffia, a big market-day to each unit. Thus Okamu unit observes the big *Eke*, Ania unit the big *Orie*, Ohafor unit the big *Afọ*, and Isiama the big *Nkwọ* market-day. Each big market-day, of course, occurs once in eight days. The four small market-days are left open to be used by the smaller villages in each unit. The result of the duplication is that the Ohaffia, like the other Ibo, have one minor week of four days (*izù ntà*) and one major week of eight days (*izù ukwu*).

The fact that each big market-day comes once in eight days makes the big market-days more important and more profitable, for it will be possible for all the villages in each unit to attend the big market held in the big village in their own unit, or the big markets of other units. For instance, it will be possible for Ohaffia villages other than those of Isiama unit to attend the big *Nkwọ* market of Ebem village in Isiama, and similarly, it will be possible for villages other than those in Okamu unit to attend the big market in Okoni in Okamu. Each village, none the less, as of right, has its own market-place and its own market-day, however small the village.

There is ample scope in this arrangement for co-operation as well as for competition in each unit as well as within Ohaffia as a community. What adds to the relative importance of almost every village is the fact that there are small-scale village specializations in certain market commodities. One village may be noted for making, or marketing, the best brooms, baskets, or pestles, another

[27] Green, 1947, p. 37 n. 2.

for better puddings or for raising better vegetables of one kind or another. It all boils down, as Miss Green has said, to the possession by one village of an art which the next door village does not have.[28]

Social objectives. As in other Ibo groups,[29] there is a great deal of rivalry in Ohaffia among related or closely situated groups in local affairs. Every village boasts the possession of whatever its neighbours happen not to have. Green's residence in Umueke Agbaja, for example, was a thing to boast of there. 'We use you to boast with. If you go away the people outside will mock at us.'[30] As we have seen, the scope for rivalry in Ohaffia as well as for co-operation is seen in the various attempts which villages in a given unit make to launch local projects in competition against the next door village even in the same unit.

In 1962 Amaekpu village in Isiama, in competition for 'progress' against Elu, Ebem, and Okagwe (all in Isiama unit), was raising funds among its own citizens to enlarge their Afo market against the wishes of the local council which had already budgeted for the development of the big *Nkwo* market at Ebem. The site at Ebem, although central, is small, and Amaekpu had offered to put its market at the disposal both of the Isiama unit and the whole of Ohaffia.

In the same year the same village, Amaekpu, was making efforts to attract to itself the new hospital which the Regional Government was planning to build for Ohaffia. It proceeded to offer a site quite in advance of a final decision which the Regional Government alone could make as to where in Ohaffia the hospital should be located. It did not see why the new hospital should not be sited at Amaekpu which 'progress' seemed to have by-passed. It was in this same village that a new building-site was marked out a little outside the village in order to encourage the building of modern houses away from the crowded huts in the village itself. This represented the first attempt in Ohaffia at town planning by the citizens themselves. It was seen, as indeed it was, as 'progress'.

Other areas where there is scope for inter-village rivalry are in the building, running, and maintaining of village schools. As in Agbaja, according to Miss Green, there is in Ohaffia rivalry among villages of the same unit to persuade the Presbyterian Mission to start new schools in one village rather than in another, however ill-advised on economic and other grounds this might be. And even

[28] Green, 1947, p. 39.   [29] Ibid., p. 13.   [30] Ibid., p. 29.

where villages in one unit each have their own schools, there is still competition amongst the villages as to which village school would score over the others in one respect or another.

Thus at Ama Ngwu in Okamu unit the Presbyterian school there has been made a non-fee-paying school by the villages who have agreed to pay the fees for every child, as well as pay the school staff. This gesture is said to indicate a more progressive outlook. It was a thing to boast of in Ama Ngwu. It was the first and is still the only non-fee-paying school in Ohaffia.

In this same spirit of mutual rivalry, many villages in Ohaffia choose to build their own schools, then afterwards to invite the Scottish Mission to staff and run them on their behalf. Most villages in Ohaffia initially would make their own 'motor' roads too, which later would be taken over by the local council. They also build the small wooden bridges which one encounters on such roads. Thus modern needs such as we have been discussing, in addition to the more traditional ones, have become generally accepted in Ohaffia community life as the arena in which traditional rivalries and co-operation among the villages are now staged.

The Territorial Structure of Amafia: a Primary Division of Amaekpu Village

We cannot speak of the primary divisions of an Ohaffia village as lineage groups, especially those of the larger villages. As we have already learned, there is no basis for doing so in the etymology of the names of those of the three villages discussed, namely, Elu, Ebem, and Amaekpu. And as far as I know, the four primary divisions in Amaekpu, for example, have no tradition of common ancestry, although the Ohaffia as a whole lay claim to one. We shall also see in a later chapter[31] that the irregularities[32] in the system of Ohaffia succession appear to confirm the absence of common ancestry at this level.

Even at the secondary level (i.e. the first *ndi*-level), Ndi Ofali in Amafia, for example, do not say that they are genealogically related to the seven other secondaries of Amafia (Fig. 1c). The claim of Ndi Ofali that they are Amafia's most senior 'compound'

---

[31] See Chapter VIII.
[32] i.e. from the point of view of the kinship ideology of the general Ibo.

is based, they say, upon priority of settlement (*su pe* = 'clearing') in Amaekpu before the others subsequently joined in.[33]

I should now go on to discuss the structure on the ground of Amafia. Certainly one of the most vivid impressions which the observer is likely to carry away from a first visit to Ohaffia is the very compact and crowded arrangement of villages and huts,

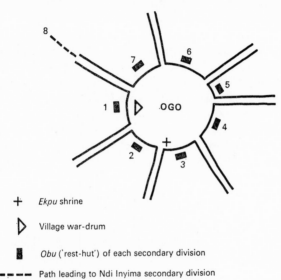

+   *Ekpu* shrine

▷   Village war-drum

▮   *Obu* ('rest-hut') of each secondary division

━ ━ ━ ━   Path leading to Ndi Inyima secondary division

FIG. 2. Territorial Structure of Amafia Primary Division of Amaekpu Village

particularly the six largest villages which carry between them the bulk of the population of Ohaffia. The spread of these villages over the broken, sparsely wooded ridge is such that not one of them stands at more than an average distance of four miles from the next. Elu, Ebem, and Amaekpu, for example, stand at less than two from one another. From the air each village would be seen to consist of very low huts, strung out in unbroken rows as if from an instinctive urge of self-defence against a danger that was once real and constant to the inhabitants. The observer cannot but feel that

[33] Idika's Diary, dated 12 July 1926, reproduced as the Appendix here, shows that patrilineages in Ohaffia could also be founded independently although they remain attached to the group which is described here as 'secondary unit'. Ndi Uyo patrilineage in Ndi Ofali 'secondary unit', in Amafia 'primary', Amaekpu village, is an example.

this crowded arrangement of Ohaffia villages and huts must be a protective response to a turbulent frontier environment. This feeling is strengthened when we take a close look at the structure of almost any of the village primary divisions like Amafia (Fig. 2). At the heart and centre of Amafia stands the central meeting-place, *ogo*. From the *ogo* the tertiary divisions radiate outwards like the spokes of a wheel (Fig. 2) and terminate towards the surrounding bush. This radial arrangement gives the entire primary unit the look of an irregular circle.

Standing on the periphery of the *ogo*, the central meeting-place, and at the head of each tertiary, are the big 'rest-huts', called the *òbu* (Fig. 2). Each *òbu* is collectively owned by the lineage segments of the secondary unit. Apart from the *òbu*, there is at one corner of the central meeting-place a small hut in which the big village war-drum is housed. No village in Ohaffia may have more than one such drum. Theoretically therefore there will be as many villages as there are drums. Also located at another corner of the *ogo* is the all-important village shrine (Fig. 2), which generally consists of a large number of big sandstones heaped round a sacred tree. It will be seen from the foregoing that objects generally regarded as sacred, collectively owned, and used by the whole village, objects like the village drum, the village shrine, and the *òbu*, are sensibly located at the centre of the senior primary unit, on the periphery of the central meeting-place (Fig. 2).

Now to take a closer look at the structure of the tertiary territorial unit, this, to start with, resembles the sector of a circle, and consists largely of unbroken rows of huts which run radially from the *ogo* towards the bush behind (Fig. 2). In between each paired row of huts lies a path (*ezi*) that leads straight into the *ogo*, emptying directly behind the appropriate 'rest-hut' (*òbu*) of the tertiary group of compounds. The hind end of the path passes through the bush surrounding the primary unit. The bush separates one territorial unit from the next. Sometimes it is farmed.

Access to a tertiary unit is possible either from the *ogo* or from the bush end of the unit; it is hardly likely and sometimes impossible from any other direction. This means that once one finds oneself in the path one becomes effectively trapped, retreat being possible only by continuing in the direction of the *ogo* or by returning towards the bush. It can therefore be imagined that should the need to defend a village primary arise, all that would need to be done would be to block the two ends of the path as one would a bridge.

Doors open into the paths between the paired rows of huts. A first visitor to an Ohaffia 'tertiary' is bound to experience the disquieting feeling of being watched by scores of eyes from behind the interiors of huts on either side of him, unable to see them himself. For such a visitor there might be the strong temptation to look over his shoulder now and again as if to assure himself that he is not being shadowed. The feeling is one of apprehension or of some danger coming as it were from all sides. Most primaries in Ohaffia are structured this way, with the result that each such unit presents the appearance of a primitive military garrison with the surrounding bush serving as a 'moat'. The one essential purpose of this kind of residential structure is effective protection and defence against surprise attack. No foe would find it easy to extricate himself if trapped within such a maze of unbroken rows of huts.

This peculiar structure of Ohaffia villages exhibits a marked contrast to those of the more settled Ibo communities, especially the non-frontier Ibo groups. In the latter cases the hut-units are largely dispersed or so arranged that each such unit is surrounded by its own garden bush, with its own path leading into it.[34] Frequently the huts within it are walled in. Clearly the factor underlying this latter kind of village configuration is different from that underlying the Ohaffia pattern. The primary factor would appear to be the need for each hut-unit to be self-sufficient in terms of subsistence although this is not always achieved. External threat in these cases may no longer be a living fear, as it was until recently in the Ohaffia type, and must have ceased to be so for a very long time indeed. Such communities have settled down.[35] Walls built round a hut-unit are probably meant to prevent goats or sheep from destroying food-plants, or just to encumber thieves but not to protect the huts against a mass assault from an enemy group.

In the more settled Ibo groups, as the unit grows, portions of the garden bush are taken up and again walled in. Alternatively, a budding-off may occur if further appropriation of garden bush becomes a crucial factor for its survival as a group, or becomes a

---

[34] This is typical among the Nnewi Ibo in Onitsha Province.
[35] Cf. Jones (1949, p. 310) on the Cross River Ibo who 'can be said to be in transition from the colonizing to the consolidating stage'.

source of dispute. Dispersed village structures of this latter kind, unlike the Ohaffia type, are more easily adaptable to change. Large modern houses can be built within the original territorial unit without wholesale damage done to the traditional over-all village structure. On the other hand, it is this sort of damage that can so easily be done to Ohaffia settlement pattern. Modern motor roads and streets have in fact done such damage to the traditional structure of one or two villages in Ohaffia.

Today, in Ohaffia, in order to avoid the building of big modern houses inside a village, or because such big houses in any case cannot be contained in the existing structure of the tertiary units, adaptation of this kind to social change takes two possible forms. One is still to build in modern house-style but at the same time conforming to the Lilliputian size of the traditional Ohaffia village hut. But to do this would be pointless and wasteful of means and material, and would amount to no useful adaptation if it is meant to replace as well as improve upon the old. And to build a big modern house within the framework of the traditional structure of a village tertiary in Ohaffia would not only produce an incongruous result and effect, but worse still would permanently encroach upon the land space of a close relative. The other alternative adaptation to change, which has in fact been adopted by Amaekpu village, is the opening of new building sites on land not far from the old village. Such new sites are parcelled out in plots of urban specifications, usually 50 feet by 100 feet. These are then sold to the sons of Amaekpu abroad or at home who can afford to buy and build on them according to the demands of modern standards in style, size, and taste.

House Structure and House Allocation in Ohaffia

A young British administrator in charge of the Bende District in which Ohaffia country is located commented in his report in 1931 that is was 'difficult to demarcate the "families" '[36] in an Ohaffia village. So far, from what we have learned about the structure of the primary as well as the secondary units of Ohaffia village, it is easy to see how this difficulty would arise, huts being built in unbroken rows. But the manner of hut allocation would reveal how the elementary family lives on the ground. The elemen-

[36] 'Intelligence Report on Ebem Court Area, Ohaffia Clan', National Archives, Enugu.

tary family unit would consist of a husband, a wife, and their children. In Ohaffia each adult member of either the elementary or the polygynous family unit would as a rule have one living-room and one bedroom to himself or, if a woman, to herself.[37] Although huts are generally paired in continuous parallel rows with a path between each pair of such rows, all huts invariably are single-room

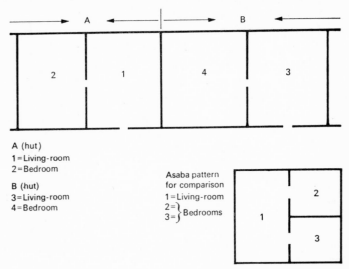

A (hut)
1 = Living-room
2 = Bedroom

B (hut)
3 = Living-room
4 = Bedroom

Asaba pattern
for comparison
1 = Living-room
2 =⎫
3 =⎭ Bedrooms

FIG. 3. Ground-plan of village hut

huts. Where there are more than two rooms in a hut, these are joined in single file, end to end like the segments of a bamboo stem, as shown in Fig. 3. It will be very unusual in Ohaffia to find two rooms of a traditional hut juxtaposed as in an Asaba hut (Fig. 3). When need for more rooms arises, as usually happens when bachelors marry or married men take additional wives, a double row of huts separated by a path is preferred. This kind of layout is in line with the over-all structure of the village primary divisions as described earlier on.

We now turn to Fig. 4; members of a simple elementary family, comprising husband, wife, and children, have rooms allocated to them in the following manner, whereas of course male adults live in separate huts from female adults. A husband therefore would

37 Cf. Green's remark (1947, p. 18) that it caused surprise among the Ibo that an English house had so many inhabitants.

occupy the hut in the paired row opposite his wife's hut, that is Fig. 4M, while his wife and children, on the other hand, would live in rooms (1) and (3) in Fig. 4F, that is, the hut opposite her husband's. She too must have a living-room and a bedroom to herself. As a rule she and her young children, irrespective of their

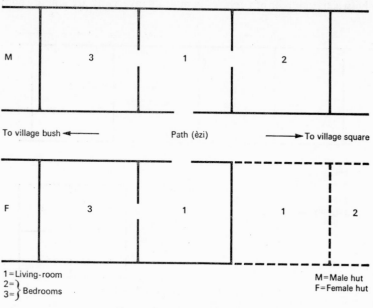

1 = Living-room
2 =
3 = } Bedrooms

M = Male hut
F = Female hut

FIG. 4. Layout of village huts

sex, would sleep in the same hut. In practice the age and the sex of a child would affect this position. An unmarried grown-up daughter, or one divorced and returned home, or widowed but not remarried, would have her own room in a female hut. But a male child, if still suckling or under seven years, would sleep in the mother's hut. Older male children sleep with senior adult males in their huts until they are of an age to live in separate huts, which they do at about the age of sixteen to eighteen years.

In the case of a polygynous family, when more than one wife is present, then the allocation of huts will be as in Fig. 4F, in which case the end hut in broken lines is occupied by the second wife. She, with her children, is given her own living-room and a bedroom, end to end to her co-wife's hut. Huts in Ohaffia grow lineally.

An extended family, say, of two male full siblings, named A and B, both of them married and with children, would abide by the same principle of hut allocation and layout, i.e. the husbands' row of huts being parallel to and facing their wives' row, as in Fig. 4. If the two brothers have a male half-sibling, C, who is also married, then C's hut is more likely to stand end to end to either A's or B's hut, not usually between the huts of the two full siblings. But no immutable rule applies in this case. But C's wife would normally have her hut facing her husband's. Since C is of the same generation as his two half-siblings, A and B, his hut would face the same common path which the huts of A and B face. But if C, on the other hand, is a generation older or younger than A and B (in which case they would not be siblings but would belong to the same minimal lineage segment), his hut is more likely to back those of A and B, facing a different path which might well be the path between the huts of members of the one extended family to which he belongs.

It follows therefore that where two parallel rows of huts stand back to back with no path between them, this would imply that although the family groups may be related, the relationship is more distant than when their rows of huts face each other as in Fig. 4. This, on the whole, is the practice. But it sometimes happens that lineage segments with no direct descent links with others would be found living in a given secondary unit. Their line of huts is generally demarcated from the next only by their shrines which are seen to punctuate the paths.

Fission of the Residential Unit

In the past, as at present, any male could leave his own residential patrilineage unit and his own village to go to start his own line side by side with some other lineage group either in the same or in another Ohaffia village, or among a group believed to be related to or friendly with the Ohaffia.[38] In any of these cases, although the immediate cause for change of residence might range from intolerable interpersonal relations with others of his own group to serious misfortunes of one kind or another, especially if these came in quick succession, the direction in which he might move would generally be decided by ties of kinship through a female,[39]

---

[38] See the Appendix, pp. 124–7. On residential patrilineages see Ch. V.
[39] A female head of a matrilineage can absorb the family of a sister's son.

or by a strong bond of long-standing friendship remembered or stored in lineage traditions. But it is not unknown that such permanent changes of residence, which amounted to contracting out of one's own kin group permanently, could also be prompted by adventure with all the hopes and risks that this might have entailed in the past.

Cases of lineage movements were remembered, although these might have occurred several generations ago. Guest lineages often feel isolated in the manner of all out-groups, and they usually keep to themselves. But, whatever the measure of the social distance between them and the host lineages, this distance does not prevent full participation on the normal day-to-day activities of the lineage of their adoption, and usually, too, such guest lineages do not object to being called by the names of the founders of their host lineages.[40] All the same, they usually stand, as the Ohaffia people say, 'on one leg'.

Fission may also occur within the village. When living space becomes scarce or is no longer available inside the primary or secondary units, expansion would, for example, normally take place at the bush end of units which need the space. The nascent lineage usually would, though not always, plant itself directly behind its ancestral secondary unit. In Fig. 2 the secondary unit numbered (8) was originally a daughter lineage which budded off from one of the secondary units in Amafia. This lineage group has now matured into a full secondary division. The arrangement of huts in this young unit reflects the same basic principle of self-defence, like the main primary itself. Within it are squares within squares of huts built in continuous rows. Entry into it is through a single side-gate by its own *òbu*. It lacks an open square of its own, but as it is still part of the primary unit of Amafia, it is entitled to the use of the *ogo*.

Shrines

Quite often shrines belonging to tertiary units are seen to punctuate paths, and this would usually indicate both the physical end, as we have earlier noted, in terms of space, of each such unit and

[40] The Uyo Ukpai Eze compound in Amaekpu village has two such guest lineages 'living with' them. The one lineage came from Asaga village in Ohaffia, which lies three miles or so from Amaekpu. The other lineage came from an unnamed village. There are numerous instances of guest lineages of this sort in most villages in Ohaffia.

the beginning of another of the same category. In almost every case the shrine of a tertiary unit consists of heaped stones arranged round a special tree (*egbò*).[41] The tertiary divisions do not have common shrines but all of them together own an *òbu* instead, where their ancestral monuments are kept. But again the *òbu* will be in the charge of the most senior tertiary group of the secondary unit in which it is located, although in fact it is usually acknowledged as a common ancestral monument by all.

There are also household shrines to be found, but these stand out of the way and close by the huts of the most senior of the extended families owning it. Unlike the shrines which belong to tertiary groups, these consist of small clay pots with wide open mouths, half-filled with earth and bits of white chalk, and some unidentifiable odds and ends, with the inevitable stains of sacrificial blood.

In quite a different category are shrines which consist of the ancestral pots (*ùdùdù*)—the most sacred objects in all Ohaffia. The pots are raised as monuments to the memory of male and female ancestors alike, and are normally sacrificed to in ritual homage. Male ancestral pots, unlike the pots of female ancestors, are kept in the open or in thatched huts, which stand in the paths as close as possible to the original spot where the hut of the founder of the senior local unit is believed to have stood. Quite often too one observes such huts directly behind the *òbu* of the village secondary unit. This location normally would point to the antiquity of the founder's arrival in the place. Village secondary units generally grow from the central meeting-place (*ogo*). This would mean in theory that the further away any particular group of male ancestral pots is located from the *òbu* of a given 'secondary', the younger its founder in the absolute scale of lineage seniority.

41 Its botanical name is *Newbouldia laevis*. It is described by J. M. Dalziel as 'a common tree around fetish groves and shrines. Amongst the Ibos it is more or less sacred or symbolic, often planted in small groves in front of the chief's house (Basden). Amongst the Ekoi and Ibibio it is a symbol of deities, and a cutting or sapling is always brought from the old town to the site of a new one' (J. M. Dalziel, *The Useful Plants of West Tropical Africa*, London, 1948, p. 445).

IV

OHAFFIA POLITICAL SYSTEM

AMONG the Ohaffia and the three Cross River Ibo communities of Ada, Abiriba, and Abam, to whom the Ohaffia claim to be related, the regulation of political relations in the village is the responsibility of age-based associations. This responsibility is shared. In Ohaffia, as in these other groups, the associations are constituted on the two principles of *age* and *selection*. By the age principle, boys and girls are grouped into age-sets when they are about three years old. Grouping at this level is informal and is repeated at three-yearly intervals for each new batch of three-year-olds. As new age-sets emerge, the ones before them automatically move up without any formal initiation rituals. Later, in young adulthood, two (or if demographically inadequate, three) of the sets become formally recognized as two opposed age-sets with specific functions. The senior of the two sets is termed *ùkè jì ogò* (literally 'age-set which holds the place'), and the junior simply *ùkè*.[1]

About ten years later, the senior of the two organizes itself into a formal association, *Akpan*, and drops the term *uke ji ogo*, which its junior, the waiting rival age-set and the former *uke*, takes over. This process of handing over of status is repeated down the line from age-set to age-set. And up the line, immediately above *Akpan*, an age-based association called *Umuaka* is encountered. At this

---

[1] *Ùkè* in Ibo means 'a stumbling-block' or 'an obstacle in one's path'. When the term is applied to the junior of two age-sets, it has the connotation of 'the opposition' or 'the left hand'. *Ùkè* set is also described in Ibo as 'the impatient ones', for they are, as it were, poised, waiting to take over from the senior set, the *ùkè jì ogo*, which was once an *ùkè* too. Among the Asaba Ibo, the senior of the two age-sets is termed *ọ̀gbọ̀*, and the junior, *ùkè*. In their thinking, the Asaba regard *ọ̀gbọ na* ('and') *ùkè* (always mentioned as a pair) as evil in the same sense in which they are regarded as 'an obstacle' to one's ambitions, hopes, and plans. The Ibo try to ward off this obstacle by the use of such statement as '*Ọgbọ n'ùkè emèna m̀*' (literally 'May senior age-set and junior age-set not do anything to me'). G. I. Jones states that 'the North Eastern Ibo [also] use the term *ọgbọ* for an age set and reserve *uke* for a quasi-age association . . .'. See his 'Ecology and Social Structure among the North Eastern Ibo', *Africa*, xxxi (1961), 130.

level of grading, the second principle applies; this means that *Umuaka* members are recruited by *selection* from the previous *Akpan*. Selection is made on the basis of certain criteria which will be discussed later. Above *Umuaka* is yet the body of old men called *Ndi Ichin*, or 'the elders', who are living remnants, so to speak, of retired *Umuaka* members. Although no longer as active as when they were *Umuaka*, *Ndi Ichin* as a body remains an association. This sequence of age-grading in Ohaffia is represented in Fig. 5.

FIG. 5. *Age-based Associations in Ohaffia*

	Age range	Name	Recruitment
1.	16–25	*Ŭkè*	Age alone
2.	26–35	*Ŭkèj̀ogó*	,,
3.	36–45	*Akpan*	,,
4.	46–55	*Umuaka*	Selection
5.	56+	*Ndi Ichin*	Survival from *Umuaka*

It follows that at any one period of about ten years[2] there are three male age-based associations in office controlling governmental powers in the village. At the base of the scale is *Akpan* which comprises men of about 36 to 45 years whose duties are police-like. Next comes the most powerful of the three, *Umuaka*, comprising men ranging in age from 46 to 55 years. At the top are *Ndi Ichin*, 'the elders', some of whom will be 56, some 65 or more. (I should stress the arbitrariness of these chronological age-categories.) I must point out too that the model as set out in the diagram and the text applies in full only to *Ohaeke* villages, as the others lack *Umuaka*. In these others, *Umuaka* is replaced by *Akpan* which then becomes accountable to the *Ndi Ichin* of these villages.

In addition to *Akpan*, *Umuaka*, and *Ndi Ichin*, there are two other agencies in the village which have some measure of governmental responsibility. One of these is *Ikpirikpe*, a women's association, the counterpart of the all-male *Umuaka*. The other is *Ama àlà*, the village assembly, an informal *ad hoc* body which cannot properly be called an association. Finally, there is the village-head, *Ezè ogò* (literally 'king of the place'). The part that associations and the village assembly play in the regulation of political relations

[2] Fig. 5 uses a conventional ten-year cycle. In reality the period varies from seven to ten years, depending upon the demographic factor of the number of people available for recruitment.

in an Ohaffia village, including the political role of the *Ezè ogó*, is considered below.

Ùkè *and* Ukèjìogó *Age-sets*

The two junior age-sets of *Ùkè* and *Ùkèjìogó* perform such ordinary village tasks as the cleaning of village-paths and market-places, and the carrying of mud bricks from the spot where these are prepared to building-sites,[3] and a few other tasks mentioned below. Generally, members of *ùkè* and *ùkèjìogó* are still regarded as minors by the adult public in the sense that they have not yet come of age and can be let off for taking certain liberties like trespassing, or pilfering coconut, which are ordinarily denied to members of older age-sets. However, among themselves, sanctions obtain, and fines are imposed upon members for misdemeanours and for failing to participate in a communal task and not sending a substitute.[4]

The Role of Akpan

By Ibo age-reckoning, the members of *Akpan* would be regarded as still in the prime of their youth, although by Western European standards they will be in their early middle age. The role of *Akpan* in the village bears a direct relation to this mode of Ibo estimation of age. Thus the members of *Umuaka* (the men's association immediately senior to *Akpan*, and the most powerful governmental body in the village), being much older than those of *Akpan*, do not carry out the enforcement of their own decisions in person. To do this is the main responsibility of *Akpan*.

Akpan arrests offenders in their houses (*wara*, literally 'catch unawares') and it promulgates *Umuaka* edicts like those prohibiting fishing out of season, or doing so at night, or collecting firewood when the ban prohibiting this is yet to be lifted. It also announces the day of the 'week' when *ùkè* and *ùkèjìogó* will, for example, be required to bridge streams, or when *Akpan* members themselves will be required to keep watch over the village farms or over the village itself if there have been cases of robbery, or rumours of it around.

---

[3] S. R. Smith, 'The Ibo People: A Study of the Religion and Customs of a Tribe in the Southern Provinces of Nigeria', Unpublished manuscript.
[4] Ibid., p. 203.

When offenders are visited by *Akpan*, they are first required to pay what might be called a 'summons fee' or *ima nzu* ('rubbing with white chalk') which usually does not exceed 5p. *Akpan* members can seize the offender's property usually by catching any fowls or goats in sight around the offender's hut,[5] and can retain such property until their demands are met or the property is forfeited. The animals so seized are not likely to belong to the offender in person, and pressure from the real owner invariably makes the offender speedily meet the demands of *Umuaka* through *Akpan*. Sometimes appeals may be made.

As we have seen, recruitment into *Akpan* is by recognizing *ùkèjìogò* age-set which is waiting to take the place of *Akpan* whose tenure of office has expired. *Akpan* has two leaders, not selected from among themselves but from members of the ruling *Umuaka*. And they are not the same people who are the leaders of *Umuaka*. The two leaders are called *Eze Akpan*, and both are secular leaders. One is the custodian of the dance instruments, the masked dancer's net-costume, the wooden dance-sword, the staff, and the gong (*ogelè*). The other presides over *Akpan* meetings. Both leaders must be men of good repute and will keep their office for as long as they maintain their good reputation. Loss of office as a result of some form of public scandal was reported to have occurred in the past. The one other office-holder is the *ògà*, who, like his counterpart in *Umuaka*, serves members on festive occasions.

Akpan is widespread in Ohaffia, and, as already pointed out, it takes over the responsibilities of *Umuaka* where the latter does not exist. In Ohaffia thinking, it ranks second to *Umuaka*.

Umuaka and *Akpan* retire or rather hand over to the next set of age-groups at the same time after a tenure lasting up to ten years. This means that the youngest member of the retiring *Akpan* who came into office at about the age of 35 years will be about 45, and the oldest will be about 55, both ready to become members of *Umuaka* if selected. The youngest member of the retiring *Umuaka* who was 45 years on becoming a member, will be 55 on retiring, he becomes a 'young' *Ndi Ichin*, so to speak, while the oldest member will be over 65 years at the end of his tenure. There is thus usually some overlap in age and membership between *Ndi*

---

[5] This is a common method of dealing with offenders in Iboland. See Meek, 1937, pp. 199 and 249.

Ichin and *Umuaka*, on the one hand, and between *Umuaka* and *Akpan*, on the other, and so down the age-scale.

The two principles of *age* and *selection* operating in the Ohaffia political system make it difficult to separate or define clearly the nature of the agencies in governmental control because these agencies too have the characteristics of age-sets as well as of associations. *Ùkèjìogò* (an age-set) becomes *Akpan* (an association) only by formal recognition as we have seen. The members of *Akpan* however become *Umuaka* (an association) by selection. And those members of *Umuaka* who survive when *Umuaka* retires go on to become *Ndi Ichin*.

The Role of Umuaka

In the eight *Ọhaeke* villages where alone *Umuaka* associations exist, each such village association is an autonomous government body, independent of the others in the other villages. Its members are recruited from *Akpan* on the basis of character and achievement, and the recruitment is the responsibility of the retiring *Ndi Ichin*. One criterion of achievement is the ability to maintain full stacks of yams,[6] generally demonstrated when a man takes the *ike ọba* (literally 'tying the stacks') title.[7] The candidate for *Umuaka* membership must have also lived a life that has so far been above village reproach. He must not, for example, have been known to be 'two-handed', that is, to be a thief, or to be given to deceit, bad debts, lying, loose living, or intemperance.

Although its membership is selected on the basis of character and achievement, *Umuaka* as an association, is not graded. It has

---

[6] Meek has the following to say about the place and significance of the yam in Ibo society. 'The staple food-crop of the Ibo is the yam, and all other crops are merely subsidiary. Much of the social and religious life of the people, therefore, centres around the cultivation of the yam. There are yam festivals, yam deities, and yam titles' (Meek, 1937, p. 16). Meek goes on to say that among the Ibo 'a man's social prestige depends to a great extent on the number of yams he is able to display . . .' (ibid., p. 17). The Ibo consider the stealing of yams such a serious social crime that in olden times, the thief would be required, in some parts of Iboland 'to drink sasswood . . .' (ibid., p. 156), or to hang himself (ibid., p. 217). An Ibo may feel so strongly about his yams that he could kill the goat caught eating his yams (ibid., p. 229). Also, in certain parts of Iboland, a dead man will ritually be given big healthy yams in the hope that on his return to Earth his yams would be as fine as the ones he was given (ibid., p. 303).

[7] This is a yam title in Ohaffia which can be taken for a child by his father, in which case the candidate will not be required to take the title again.

no orders, and no hierarchy of office-holders, although it has its officials who perform specific duties. No women are recruited.

Its two leaders are elected by general agreement, later approved by the *Ndi Ichin*. The approval is usually a formality. Long before it becomes formally necessary to elect the leaders, the candidates might already have emerged as strong or obvious choices through their own achievements or through their personal qualities for leadership in secular or in magico-religious matters. They must also be able and reasonable men in society. *Ndi Ichin* would show their support by attending any public ceremony arranged by *Umuaka* to acknowledge their leaders. The leaders are called by the same title, *Ezè Umuaka*, but are distinguished from each other by their respective duties, in the one case secular, and in the other, ritual. When it becomes necessary to distinguish one from the other, the secular leader is then specifically called *Ezè Umuaka*, and the ritual one, *Ezè Nkwà*.[8]

The secular leader presides over the meetings. It is his responsibility to summon them at the request of the *Ndi Ichin*, or by a deputation of *Akpan* members, or on his own initiative in the event of any happening which in his opinion or on the advice of other members would necessitate meeting. He is the keeper of the horn (*òpì*), one of the two insignia of office which the association owns. It is he alone who should normally blow this horn, or can ask someone else to do so. The horn is very rarely used, except when incidents of grave import occur, like the death of a notable, or a serious breach of the village peace.

Eze Nkwa, the ritual leader, is the priest of the association and the custodian of the association's big 'medicine', *Ijiji ebè* (literally 'no fly would dare to perch'). He has the responsibility of guarding the ritual well-being of the association, and keeps the association from being ritually tainted.[9] There is one other official, the steward or *òga*, whose job it is, as in the case of *Akpan*, to share out drinks, or tobacco, or kola among members.

Umuaka meetings are conducted in the open and generally by day in the *òbu* ('rest-hut') of the 'tertiary unit' of the village, the

---

[8] *Nkwà* in Ohaffia refers to a dance; if it is a big ritual one, it is then called *oke* (literally, 'male' *nkwa*).

[9] Tainting here refers to abominations against the Earth (*iru àlà*) for which, in every case, the Earth (*àlà*) needs to be sacrificed to. See Meek, 1937, p. 27.

unit recognized by the rest of the village as the most senior by priority of settlement. *Umuaka* meetings are not open to non-members except by invitation or by special permission. If the visitor is a stranger, a small fee of 10p is demanded 'for drinks or snuff'. And even so the visitor must enter the *òbu* barefoot, and be seated at a good distance from members.

The main responsibilities of *Umuaka* are to see that village peace is maintained and to reconcile the general interest of the village community with the exercise of the rights of its units and of individuals. *Umuaka* has the power to place restrictions upon the exercise of these rights should they conflict with the interest and the needs of the village community. As already mentioned, it is the responsibility of *Umuaka* to prohibit fishing in village streams at certain seasons, and during the fishing period to prohibit doing so at night. Such common rights as the hunting and the trapping of wild animals, cutting sticks, or strings, collecting firewood or mushrooms, or palm fruits from wild oil-palm trees in the bush, or digging clay for domestic uses, and the general exploitation of natural resources of the land and of streams, provided that these do not infringe private rights, are guaranteed by the village *Umuaka*.

It is also the special responsibility of the village *Umuaka* to protect the lives of its citizens against public assault or injury by their fellow villagers or next-door village neighbours. But it is said that, although in the past *Umuaka* used to wield the ultimate sanction of death, it was sometimes unable to prevent a village from avenging the death of any of its members killed by a man from a different village. This was said to be rare.

Public mischiefs like robbery with violence, especially if this was committed against a non-Ohaffia community with whom the village had an *ukwuzi* relationship, constituted a serious offence against the authority of *Umuaka*. Other offences against *Umuaka* are calling a fellow Ohaffia a slave, and publicly disowning a kinsman.

Legal sanctions for offences depended upon the seriousness of such offences. But sanctions ranged from fines (in addition to the penalty of restoring things stolen or damaged) to public ridicule and disgrace. It is said that in the past a thief would be stripped naked, dressed in rags or twigs, his face blackened with soot, and then paraded through the village high streets while being made to dance to the tune of an *ògbèrè*[10] song accompanied by drumming and singers.

Banishment was also used as a sanction against a persistent offender. Especially insensitive or hardened offenders were sold as slaves. *Umuaka* also used to wield the ultimate sanction of death, usually by requiring the offender to kill himself by jumping from the top of an oil-palm or coconut-palm. This he was usually made to do at night, before the first crow of the cock. The sentence of death was in principle irreversible and beyond appeal. But in practice appeals were sometimes possible and were made to *Ohaeke*. These were only likely to be attempted successfully if strong opposition or pressure could be mounted because of strong doubt of the offender's guilt, or if some vested interest in his death was suspected, or if the offender was a citizen of considerable influence.

Such offences as incest, or adultery with a patrikin's wife, are called *ìru àlà* ('abominations of the Earth'). These are punished with the consent of *Umuaka* by the women. They dump village refuse at the doorsteps of the male and the female offenders.[11] Ritual offences are the more difficult to discern. Examples are stealing from a shrine (this is of rare occurrence), or a woman becoming pregnant within the period of mourning her dead husband. These offences, however, are not considered to be offences against *Umuaka* and, in any case, are generally believed to be capable of invoking their own vengeance. All the same, offenders are tried, and are required to procure restoration by ritual cleansing.

The village public, consisting of women, children, and men who are not members, hold *Umuaka* in some awe. There is no reason to suppose that this is simulated. If, for example, members of the village *Umuaka* are on the march, which they do in single file and always in dead silence, with each member carrying his staff of office (*ńkpa*), the only insignia or badge of membership one possesses, no villager, however distinguished, must touch or speak to any member of the moving body, much less cross its path.

In villages where *Umuaka* does not exist, its responsibilities

---

[10] *Ògbèrè* is a song in which an offender of society is ridiculed. If a thief, he may be called names and described as 'a man who wants to eat but not work'.
[11] If the male co-respondent is brought before *Umuaka*, it can, in addition to the dumping of refuse at his door-step by women, punish the man.

F

devolve upon the *Akpan* of such villages, but the *Akpan* associations of such villages will be under the direct authority of their
Ndi Ichin. But where *Umuaka* exists the role of *Ndi Ichin* in Ohaffia
becomes advisory only.

Ndi Ichin: '*The Elders*'

Ndi Ichin are men who because of their age have retired from
active participation in the running of the affairs of the village.
They are referred to in full as *Ndi Ichin Umuaka* ('Elders of
Umuaka'). Although no longer members of *Umuaka*, they are
sometimes invited to its meetings to advise when serious matters
are to be discussed,[12] or if there are some gifts or benefits to share.

The prestige and the influence of *Ndi Ichin* derive from the
fact that, among the Ibo generally, wisdom and knowledge of local
traditions are associated with age. When there are disputes over
lands, they are the ones to be consulted and whose evidence is
sought. In other ways their opinion can strengthen or weaken any
course of action that *Umuaka* might take. *Ndi Ichin* cite remembered precedents to support a course of action, or deny knowledge
of any, and thus may weaken or avert a particular course. As said
earlier, the role of *Ndi Ichin* is essentially advisory.

The Role of Ama àlà: '*The Village Assembly*'

A fourth body which is generally associated with the affairs of
the village is the *ad hoc* village assembly, *Ama àlà* (literally 'path
of the Earth' or 'the public meeting-place'), so called because the
village public sometimes rallies there. The role and character of
Ama àlà are the same (and it is called by the same name) in most
parts of Iboland.[13] It is convened only when very serious issues
arise, such as an untraced murder, or an external threat, or when a
new proclamation of a change in custom is to be made, or in a case
of an 'abomination of the Earth' (*iru àlà*).[14] All these are capable of
arousing public interest, or indignation, and are outside the scope
and authority of *Umuaka* of individual villages.

Ama àlà is the one body in Ohaffia (as well as in other parts of
Iboland) which can stand in the path of *Umuaka* and reverse any

[12] Cf. Meek, 1937, p. 110, where he notes that '. . . a court of *Oha* may call in
elders who are not *Oha* as assessors, if they find the matter one of difficulty'.

[13] Among the Asaba Ibo, *òbòdò* ('citizenry') is used rather than *Ama àlà*.

[14] In ordinary Ibo parlance, one is said to taint the Earth (*ru àlà*) when one is
guilty of sacrilege; incest is a grave example.

unpopular course of action set in motion by *Umuaka*. An *Ama àlà* meeting is open to all adult male citizens or to any category of age-groups who may not only attend but have the right of hearing and can contribute to the discussion freely.[15]

In theory an *Ama àlà* meeting can be convened by following the proper procedure, such as by getting the consent of *Umuaka* or through lobbying the *Ndi Ichin*. But it can spontaneously be summoned if an issue of serious import affecting a whole village or a group of villages should develop, as well as where such issues call for a consensus. There is no limitation of right to membership of the assembly and any male member of the village is free to participate in the assembly meeting of his own village, or that of any group of villages in which his village is represented.

The Ibo are generally known for their strong attachment to, and deep respect for, the principle and practice of 'direct democracy'. It is at the village assembly meetings that this disposition is so clearly, if at times so clumsily, exemplified. British administrative officials had cause to complain not so much about the Ibo love of democracy as the practice of it in Ohaffia in the early 1930s.

Every male person [one such official stated in his report] had the right to attend a meeting . . . and to speak when he so desired. This was an indisputable privilege bestowed on each individual and handed down to posterity, and such was the conservative mind of the people that any suggested modification or diversion from this rule of government would have been regarded as bordering on the ridiculous. The members of the [village] council only began to operate administratively when the subject matter of the meeting had already been discussed.[16]

The Role of Ikpirikpe: *a Women's Association*

The Ohaffia womenfolk have their own traditional law-keeping body, the nearest equivalent of the exclusively male village *Umuaka*. *Ikpirikpe*, as this body is called, is open to one female age-set. Like the equivalent young adult male sets it is called *ùkèjìogò*.

Ikpirikpe mainly runs the affairs of the adult women of the village and imitates *Umuaka* in a number of ways. For instance, it observes dead silence when on the march, and proceeds in a single file like the men. The public of non-members (here men and boys)

[15] V. C. Uchendu, *The Igbo of Southeast Nigeria*, New York, 1965, p. 41.
[16] Intelligence Report No. S.P. 10411/12, National Archives, Enugu, Eastern Nigeria, 28 Feb. 1934.

are expected to observe similar rules of 'no entry', unless by permission, when the body is meeting.

Perhaps the most interesting feature of *Ikpirikpe* is its near-absolute independence in the affairs of the village womenfolk.[17] It is the one and only body that can deal with the offences committed by women. In cases of adultery, for instance, *Umuaka* (as earlier noted) could, if the matter came before it, punish the male culprit, but would be powerless over the female accomplice. *Ikpirikpe* can mount a strong and sustained opposition against any action or decision by the men. If, for example, the menfolk ruled against cutting wood from the farm-bush too early in the season, this might be objected to by the women. In such circumstances *Ikpirikpe* can rule that village housewives should leave their homes and husbands *en masse*, abandoning all children temporarily, except suckling babies, and would not return unless their views were heard or their grievances looked into and some compromise reached.[18] This mass desertion of their homes to their own patrilineages is intended to put teeth into their objections.

The recruitment of members into *Ikpirikpe* is obviously non-lineage based, since most of them are wives and may not belong to the village in which they live. Like the members of the all-male *Umuaka*, those of the *Ikpirikpe* are selected from among women of the relevant age-based group, although in their case the range in their ages may be considerably wider (from 36 to 55+). Selection is done by the retired women elders who are not technically named as a body, as in the case of the all-male *Ndi Ichin*. The leader of the *Ikpirikpe* is called the *Ezè nwanyì* who combines the secular function of presiding over meetings, or speaking for the body, with the ritual one of initiating the planting of crops by women in the farms. Unlike the *Umuaka*, the *Ikpirikpe* is its own executor or agent, although in punishing, say, an adulterer, all the housewives, young or old, will be invited to participate in heaping refuse at the doorsteps of the adulterers.

Ezè ogó: *the Village Head*

Every Ohaffia village, unless too small (and therefore politically attached to a bigger one),[19] has a head who is called the *Ezè ogó*, whose office is not hereditary, and whose selection does not always

---

[17] Cf. Meek, 1937, pp. 200–1.   [18] Ibid., p. 201.

[19] See p. 11 of this monograph.

go by the same principle in every village. How he is chosen in the various villages in Ohaffia is fully discussed in Chapter VIII.

His role in politics is interesting in that it is not unlike that of a constitutional monarch in terms of both internal and external relations. He does not openly participate in the running of the affairs of his own village; he does not attend meetings and therefore does not preside over them; nor does he undertake any ritual duties. He is greatly respected but not regarded in any sense as a sacred functionary. What seems to matter in selecting one are the exceptional personal qualities which a candidate must have.

An *Ezè ogò*, whom I know personally, Chief Emetu of Amaekpu village, tall, athletic, and still physically strong at about 75 years of age in 1962, has the kind of personality that easily wins rather than imposes respect. He is still regarded as the best shot for many miles around.[20] In his long career as a hunter, he was said to have accounted for 'more buffalo-heads dead than alive in the bush', as well as elephants which he has a licence to hunt. He is the 'husband' (that is to say 'the terror') of such lesser game as bush-hog or antelope. He is a retired government school headmaster, a pioneer in education, not only in Ohaffia, but as far afield as Afikpo and parts of Ogoja Province.

His most useful role to his people has been as a fearless emissary: heading delegations, sometimes on behalf of the whole of Ohaffia, to government ministers and high-ranking officials of his region. Thus, as far as one could see, his duties as the village head lay in the sphere of external relations. I was told, and I believed it, that it was on account of his qualities as a person that he was chosen as the *Ezè ogò* of Amaekpu. In spite of these he was kept out of village politics. This makes him a leader of special rank among his people. Nor was he exceptional in Ohaffia. In the villages of Asaga, and Ebem, their *Ezè ogò* have comparable reputations.

Conclusion

The structure of the Ohaffia political system can, in a sense, be described as 'pyramidal'. It has a broad base which derives directly from a system of age-grade organization. From this it builds up, first by formal recognition into *Akpan*, and later by selection into

[20] At the time I visited him he was in the thick of two big projects: the building of a hospital and of a central market for Amaekpu, his village. For doing this, he had on more than one occasion come into conflict with (as he described him) 'a young, and corrupt, government official'.

Umuaka, then finally by survival into *Ndi Ichin*. Each of these is ranked above the one below it on the basis of age, but at the same time each is an association by a specific principle of recruitment. In parallel, there are the *Ikpirikpe*,[21] the female counterpart of *Umuaka*, and the village polity, *Ama àlà*, as well as the village head, *Ezè ogó*. The roles of the last two lie on the periphery of village politics.

All the governmental agencies named each act independently in their own spheres as well as in support of each other in the general village interest, and seek a consensus. The Ohaffia system seems to have struck a balance between the statelike type on the one hand (in which the possibility of tyranny is a constant threat to the rights of citizens and to the stability of the system) and, on the other, the unmodified segmentary lineage type (in which a certain instability replaces tyranny as the overriding danger both to the system and to society).[22]

Commenting on the 'stateless'/'statelike' scheme of Fortes and Evans-Pritchard,[23] on the basis of her own survey of West African societies, Paula Brown thinks that 'finer distinctions are possible and that not all these [West African] societies can be placed in one or the other of these two categories. In particular, the classification of 'stateless' societies in which associations, rather than a segmentary lineage system, regulate political relations; and it fails to distinguish different types of authority and political structure in states.'[24]

Middleton and Tait raise similar objections to the scheme. One aim of their *Tribes Without Rulers* was to improve upon the theory on which the dichotomy was based. Middleton referred to the scheme as 'out of date'.[25] In Forde's study of the Yako too we have a similar critical view:

. . . the not uncommon tendency to perpetuate a scheme of apparently

[21] The existence of *Ikpirikpe* indicates that the residential unit of village women in Ohaffia (as in other parts of Iboland) is also an organized unit.

[22] I must admit that more fieldwork on the Ohaffia political system would yield further details on age-set organization and on the relationship between the various age-sets (both male and female) as well as details of the extent to which modern political institutions have pre-empted the traditional roles of the age-based associations we have been considering.

[23] M. Fortes and E. Evans-Pritchard, *African Political Systems*, London, 1940, pp. 5 and 9.

[24] P. Brown, 'Patterns of Authority In West Africa', *Africa*, xxi (1951), 261.

[25] J. Middleton and D. Tait, *Tribes Without Rulers*, London, 1958, p. vii.

clear-cut categories that served a useful purpose would seem to have hindered general recognition that some indigenous forms of government in Africa cannot, even as a first approximation, be fitted into so simple a dichotomy. Among these are societies in which self-perpetuating associations exercise autonomous ritual power and secular authority over part or all of the population with respect to a major sphere of social life.[26]

Further comment by me would seem unnecessary. It seems clear from these writers that the Ohaffia type of political system run by age-based associations is not accommodated by the two-category scheme. The precise role of the kinship and lineage system in Ohaffia will be discussed in the next two chapters.

[26] D. Forde, *Yakö Studies*, London, 1964, p. 166.

V

OHAFFIA KINSHIP TERMINOLOGY

IN all but a few cases which are specified in the text, Ohaffia kinship terms are much the same as those of the general Ibo.[1] In those cases in the Ohaffia system in which new terms occur, or in which the Ohaffia use the same terms as occur in the general Ibo terminology differently, such usages tend to emphasize the matrilineal bias in their system. In this chapter we shall be considering Ohaffia kinship terms from Ego's standpoint as follows:

1. *Ikwu* (singular: *onye ikwù*). The term refers to the matrilineage, that is, persons who, in Fox's words, are '. . . the descendants of the original "mother" through females; her sons and daughters, the sons and daughters of her daughters and so on . . . the members of our group [here *ikwu*] will all be related to each other through females only.'[2]

The etymology of the term *ikwu* confirms the link through females. *Ikwu*, or *ekwu* in Ibo, literally means 'kitchen dish' or, in a more general sense, 'kitchen thing'. As a kinship term, it implies 'persons who eat from one dish or who eat in the same kitchen'. Even among the patrilineal Ibo, only children of one mother as a rule are supposed to eat from one dish or in the same kitchen.[3] In Ohaffia members of this group form the origins of the matrilineage. They refer to themselves as *anyi ñùrù otù arà* (literally 'we suck one breast'). The Ohaffia also say *enwegh nnà nwè nne* (literally 'one without a father has a mother'). This means that a child who

---

[1] Fig. 6 is reproduced from Ardener's article, 'The Kinship Terminology of a Group of Southern Ibo', *Africa*, xxiv (Apr. 1954), 90. His description of the Ezinihite-Ibo kinship terminology is the fullest and clearest yet available and applies to a good many patrilineal Ibo communities other than Ezinihite. My own description of the Ohaffia kinship terminology is meant to show where it contrasts with his. The numbered sections on his chart are a device whereby he distinguishes the main categories of relatives with whom Ego has to deal.

[2] R. Fox, *Kinship and Marriage*, Harmondsworth, 1967, p. 43.

[3] Ardener, 1954, p. 91.

may not know his true patrilineage, that is, a child of unknown father, must still have a matrilineage. No one in Ohaffia thus is so destitute as to lack a matrilineage.

In Ohaffia *ikwu* forms a descent category which in the general Ibo system is not recognized as such. In Fig. 6, Ardener's chart of the patrilineal system, the *ikwu* does not appear, but some of the

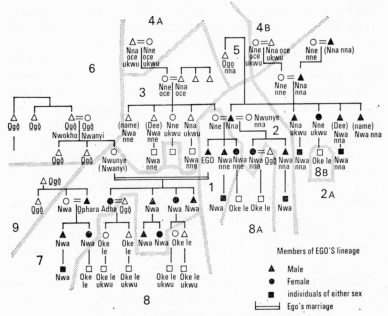

FIG. 6. Chart of Ibo Kinship Terminology Ezinihite Dialect
(after Ardener, 1954)

equivalent genealogical relatives appear in his sections 1, 3, 4A, and 7. In Ohaffia matrilineages are the exogamous units, and these are named after their ancestresses.[4] The children of male full siblings do not belong to the same matrilineage as their fathers, although the contrary is true: those of female full siblings do. Marriage is permissible between sister's son and mother's brother's daughter, or between mother's brother's son and sister's daughter, for in either case husband and wife belong to two different exogamous matrilineages, and, as we shall see, patrilineages in Ohaffia are not exogamous. Because residence in Ohaffia is patrilocal, the

---

[4] *Ekeuke* is such a matrilineage, see Fig. 9.

male members of the matrilineage are the fixed points in the net-
work of dispersed relatives in a matrilineage. The tendency to
dispersion is diminished by the mechanism of matrilateral and
patrilateral cross-cousin marriage.

Among the Ezinihite-Ibo, as in other patrilineal Ibo groups,
although Ego, as I have said earlier, obviously has the genealogical
relatives who make up the *ikwu* unit in Ohaffia, the unit in Ezinihite is not distinguished as a category. The term *àgbèrè* (or *àgbùrù*
in the Bible orthography), which literally means 'blood or hereditary link', applicable to both father's and mother's lines, could be
used in Ezinihite if the qualifier for mother, *nne*, is attached to it,
thus: *àgbùrù nne*. But *àgbùrù* could equally refer to Ego's father's
line too if the word for father, *nnà* in Ibo, is put after it, thus:
àgbùrù nnà. Both terms refer in any case to cognatic relatives. So
in actual fact, *ikwu* as a term is not applicable in Ezinihite frame
of kinship terminology. In Ohaffia the matrilineage (*ikwu*) is a
property-holding and property-inheriting group which is quite
lacking in Ezinihite[5] or in other patrilineal Ibo groups.

2. *Umudi*. This term in Ohaffia refers primarily to the children
of Ego's father by another wife than Ego's mother, such as the two
children in category 2, each of whom in Ezinihite is called by Ego
nwa nnà ('child of father', i.e. 'half-sibling'), irrespective of sex.

The term *umudi* can also be applied, as many Ibo kinship terms
usually are,[6] to include all Ego's patrikin. In either of its main
connotations it is a term bled of any tender emotions in Ohaffia
and is tinged with concealed hostility, probably even more so than
among the patrilineal Ibo groups. Members of Ego's *umudi* belong
to the category of kin from whom Ego can take a wife. Such a wife
would be referred to by her husband as *nwa nnà di* (husband's
father's daughter). The term is not reciprocal, that is, Ego would
not be called by the same term by his wife. Such marriages, among
the patrilineal Ibo are of course not permissible, and would be
regarded with horror. The application of the term *nwa nnà di* is
unknown among them. This difference and a similar one to be
indicated later is crucial to a 'diagnosis' of the existence of matriliny
in Ohaffia.

Umudi, translatable literally as 'children of mother's husband',

[5] Ardener, 1954, p. 97.
[6] E. W. Ardener, 'Lineage and Locality among Mba-Ise Ibo', *Africa*, xxix
(1959), 129.

bespeaks a gulf between Ego and his half-siblings. This parting of the ways can be seen from the fact that Ego can take a wife from among them; it is reflected too in the physical layout of lineage huts in Ohaffia where huts of the *umudi* are back to back, or are located at the end of the row, away from the huts of male full siblings, whose huts may face one another or stand adjacent to one another.

Except for the female members of this group who may marry and live away, all *umudi* are normally physically localized and, as already indicated, are the basis of the residential unit in Ohaffia, which in this respect, therefore, does not differ from the general Ibo. Like them, the Ohaffia reside in territorially based patri-lineages, although the permitting of marriage within the close patrilineal group in Ohaffia sets it off from the patrilineage in the other Ibo, as well as from the patriclan in the Yako[7] or Lo Dagaba.[8] The *umudi* (patrilineage) in Ohaffia is clearly the mirror-image of *ikwu* (matrilineage), but is not the same as *umu nna*, the strictly exogamous patrilineage of the general Ibo.

3. *Ndi nne*. This is a difficult category of Ego's matrilateral kin to describe. Literally the term means 'those related to mother'. They are broadly the mother's patrilineage. But *ndi nne* in Ohaffia must exclude all members of Ego's matrilineage (*ikwu*). *Ndi nne*, for instance (except in a very general sense), are not Ego's mother's full siblings: these are in Ego's *ikwu* (matrilineage); nor are *ndi nne* the children of Ego's female full siblings (except again in a very general sense): these too are part of Ego's *ikwu*. *Ndi nne* are what is left of Ego's mother's patrilineage after all members of Ego's *ikwu* are extracted from this residential group. This residue would consist in the first place of the children of Ego's mother's male full siblings (i.e. all children of mother's brothers); in the second place, of both male and female half-siblings of Ego's mother as well as the children of these. *Ndi nne* all fall into Ego's mother's *umudi*. Ego can take a wife from this group. We have seen that if Ego marries from his own patrilineage (*umudi*), such a woman is termed *nwa nna di*. If Ego takes a wife from his mother's *umudi* (patri-lineage) such a woman is referred to by Ego as his *nwa nne di*. Here the term *nna* (father) is replaced by *nne* (mother). However, the term *nwa nne di* is also used of a wife who is father's sister's daughter, a relative who belongs to the father's matrilineage.

---

[7] Forde, 1964, p. 95.　　　　[8] See Chapter XI.

Ardener's *ɵmɵnɛ* (or *umune* in the Ibo Bible orthography), which 'refers to the household of Ego's mother's father',[9] would in Ohaffia include Ego's *ndi nne* and some of his *ikwu* relatives. Therefore no exactly equivalent term to Ardener's *ɵmɵnɛ* (Fig. 6) exists in Ohaffia.

4. *Umù*. This term literally means 'children' (singular: *nwa*) irrespective of sex. Strict differentiation of sex can be made by the addition of words for male (*nwoke*) and for female (*nwanyì*) after the term *nwa*. Thus *nwa nwoke*, 'male child', *nwa nwanyì*, 'female child'. To Ego and his wife (to any Ibo in fact), their children are the dearest possessions to wish for or to have.

Umù refers in the first place to Ego's own children by blood or by adoption, whether or not the children are by one or more wives, or by an unmarried woman who is not Ego's wife. In the latter case ridicule and sometimes social stigma may attach to such children, who may be referred to as *umu ɔ̀yì* ('children born in friendship'). Where, however, a woman is married to another man, even if she is known to have had the children by Ego, the children are those of the legal husband.

The term *umù* has its narrowest field of reference within the above context, a context in which Ego and his children are in direct link by blood or by adoption. Application of the term beyond this is:

(i) To the children of Ego's full siblings irrespective of sex. Ego's full siblings, and the children of his male full siblings are in section 1 in Fig. 6. But if, however, the children of Ego's male full siblings are older than Ego,[10] or about the same age, then to Ego they are first *umù nne* (singular *nwa nne*, which in Ibo can also be used in the collective sense), and secondly, if of Ego's female full siblings, such children would be members of *ikwu* to Ego, a term which has been fully discussed in section 1 above.

(ii) The next application of the term *umù* among the patrilineal Ibo communities would be to the children of Ego's half-siblings. But this usage is so rare among the Ohaffia that it can generally be ignored in their kinship system. It has been pointed out earlier that in Ohaffia Ego can take a wife from among this category of kin. They use a term which literally means 'children of half-siblings' (*umù nwa nnà*). There is reluctance to apply the term *umù* (children)

---

[9] Ardener, 1954, p. 92.
[10] See ibid., p. 91, for the circumstance in which this may happen.

to persons who are potentially his wives or affines.[11] For the patrilineal Ibo, division between Ego's own children and the children of his male half-siblings occurs because they are potential rivals over patrilineage rights, but they are not potentially intermarriageable. Thus the term *umu* among the Ohaffia is more limited in reference than among the patrilineal Ibo.

In Ohaffia (but not in Ezinihite Ibo) Ego himself can also be referred to as *nwa* by his mother's full siblings, namely mother's brother or mother's sister, and the children of his mother's full siblings are, to Ego's mother, *umù* too. It may be noted that, in Ibo as a whole, *umù* is capable of being further applied outside the limits of kinship and affinal relationship; for apart from its use to assert the unity of the group, an older person can refer to any much younger person as 'my child' (*nwam*). We might also note that among the Ohaffia as among the patrilineal Ibo groups, ridicule and some stigma attaches to a childless marriage, both to the woman and to the man. The term *àgà* is applied to a barren wife. The man or husband may be referred to as *utù onwu* ('dead penis') and if he finally fails to beget a child before his death, his 'branch' (in Ibo literally *alaka*), or more correctly his 'path' (*ama*), is said to be blocked (*echie*).

5. *Umù nne.* Next to his own children in closeness of blood kinship to Ego, comes the category of relatives who are also the children of Ego's mother, Ego's full siblings. These to Ego are *umù nne* ('children of mother'; singular *nwa nne*). They are in group 1 in Fig. 6. In Ohaffia the term has a narrower range of application than it has among the patrilineal Ibo. Apart from Ego's own full siblings, the children of these are also to Ego *umù nne*, especially if they are as old or about his age. But if younger, Ego can correctly call them his *umù* (children) as we have already explained. In Ohaffia Ego cannot, must not in fact, refer to the children of mother's sisters as *umù nne*. The proper term of reference for this category of kin is *ikwu*, as has already been shown.

6. *Nwunyè.* Ego's wife is his *nwunyè*. When broken into its component parts, it is held to mean 'catch' (*nwudo*) and 'give' (*nye*), meaning in full 'give'. Since in Ohaffia Ego can take a wife

[11] Even among the patrilineal Ibo, for whom such marriages are out of the question, the term is still generally restricted in its use to Ego's own children unless 'the close unity of the whole body of relations' (i.e. Ego's children and the children of his half-siblings) needs to be asserted against a relatively more distant kin group (see Ardener, 1954, p. 91).

from his patrilineage as well as from mother's *ndi nne*, the term has a larger or wider range than among the patrilineal Ibo where the restrictions of exogamy are different.

7. *Ọgọ̀*. This term means 'affine' or 'in-law'. I suspect that the word has the same root as the word for 'gift' (*ọgọ̀*), the stem of which in Ibo is tonally and phonologically exactly the same with a *prefix* on a different tone. Among the Ibo, a good wife is appropriately referred to as a gift. Ego's affines are therefore referred to as *ọgọ̀*. In Ohaffia, as in other parts of Iboland, Ego's wife's parents, his wife's full siblings, his wife's matrilineage and patrilineage, and his wife's mother's patrilineage are all Ego's in-laws (*ọgọ̀*), as well as the in-laws (*ọgọ̀*) of Ego's own kin groups both matrilateral and patrilateral. The term *ọgọ̀* in Ohaffia can further include members of Ego's own patrilineal kin, as well as of his *ndi nne*, because of their marriage pattern. The category of affinal kinship in Ohaffia can be very close indeed in blood. It is the contrary among the patrilineal Ibo, as Ego and his wife should not belong to the same *àgbùrù* (blood-kin).

From this discussion of Ohaffia kinship terms, the following differences between the Ohaffia and the patrilineal Ibo groups have emerged:

(i) In Ohaffia, there is an exogamous matrilineage (*ikwu*) and, surprisingly for an Ibo community, the absence of an exogamous patrilineage (*umu di*). Among the patrilineal Ibo (Ezinihite, for example), the matrilineage is not a category as in Ohaffia. In the patrilineal Ibo, patrilineage is strictly exogamous, although Ego here must also not marry from *ọmọne*, his mother's patrilineage.

(ii) The marriage of patrilineal relatives even as close as half-siblings is permitted in Ohaffia. This would be an abomination (*mmeru àlà*) in Ezinihite.

(iii) Finally, the patrilineage in Ohaffia (*umudi*: *di* = husband) receives its term from a woman's viewpoint. In the patrilineal Ibo groups, the patrilineage (*umù nnà*: *nna* = father) is defined from the man's viewpoint. Similarly, in Ohaffia the terms *nwa nnà di* and *nwa nne di* are defined from the woman's point of view. Detailed discussion of some of these differences and others related to descent and inheritance are given in subsequent chapters.

VI

ASPECTS OF OHAFFIA KINSHIP

The Marriage of Close Kin

WE saw in the preceding chapter that a man can take a wife from among his own agnatic kin group in Ohaffia. Not only is he not forbidden, he may in fact be encouraged to do so. The Ohaffia in this respect say *Ayi nàmu, nuru* ('we take in marriage' whom we bear), *màkà udo* ('for amity'),[1] by which is meant peace in the home and in the patrilineage. In patrilineal Ibo groups as I have earlier observed such unions would be viewed with horror, and would in fact be regarded as incest, a sin believed to be capable of bringing disaster upon both the pair and the patrilineage.

Some variations of preferred marriage-forms as practised by the Ohaffia are shown in Fig. 7. Ego (Aa), for example, may, as in Fig. 7a, marry the daughter (Ac) of his male half-sibling.[2] The woman so married is Ego's close patrikin, the granddaughter of Ego's own father. In Ohaffia such a wife is called by her husband *nwa nnà di*, meaning, as already explained, 'husband's own half-sibling', for by extension she is to Ego, her husband, what her father is to Ego, namely *nwa nna* (father's child), a category of kinship, *umudi*, already discussed.

Secondly, as shown in Fig. 7b, Ego (Ac) can also marry the daughter of his father's male half-sibling, the same woman whom Ego's father could marry. The woman so married is still *nwa nnà di* to her husband. The two forms of marriage are still within the category of agnatic marriage, wife and husband being agnates.

Thirdly, as shown in Fig. 7c, Ego (Ac) can also take the daughter (Ca) of his father's female half-sibling as wife. Ego's father (Aa) in this case and his half-sister (Ba) are of the same mother but of different fathers; Ego's father's mother (a) was married twice, the

[1] G. Karlsson, 'On Mate Selection', in *Family and Marriage*, ed. J. Mogey, Leiden, 1963, pp. 91–2, for various motives behind mate selection.

[2] One known case was that of Iro Uduma, a teacher who married the daughter of his father's male half-sibling.

second time to (B) after the death of Ego's grandfather (A). The relationship between husband (Ab) and wife (Ba) as shown in Fig. 7*d* was even closer in a known case, where Ego's father (Aa)

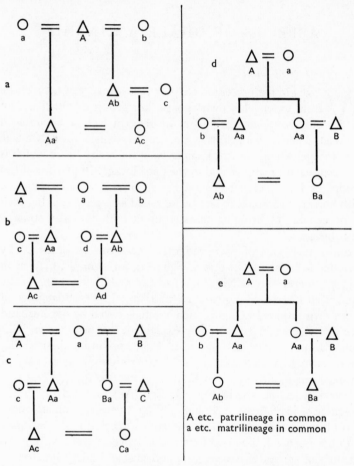

A etc. patrilineage in common
a etc. matrilineage in common

FIG. 7. Forms of preferred marriage in Ohaffia, *none* permissible among other Ibo groups

and Ego's aunt (Aa) were full siblings. The woman (Ba) so married is referred to by her husband (Ab) as *nwa nne di*, meaning 'husband's own sister'. The four types of marriage cited are permissible in Ohaffia because in no case do the spouses belong to the same matrilineage (*ikwu*). All four types of marriage comply with

the rule of matrilineage exogamy in Ohaffia. But among the patrilineal Ibo none of them is permissible. But whereas Ego cannot
marry mother's sister's daughter, because both belong to the same
matrilineage, Ego (Ba) can marry mother's brother's daughter
(Ab) in Fig. 7e, again because both husband and wife do not belong
to the same matrilineage.

In none of the different marriage types described here is *pre-
scription* a factor.[3] The point to emphasize is that in so far as these
types are not *permissible* among the patrilineal Ibo, their absence
there underlines the contrast between their marriage system and
that of the Ohaffia Ibo. In practically all the cases of preferred
marriage types in Ohaffia, the choice rests with the older people in
the particular kin group, not with the prospective spouses. The
motives of the older people would normally coincide with the
general Ibo ones. Marriage takes into account personality characteristics of the *àgbùrù* ('blood-line') of those concerned, and the social
and economic status of its members.

Wealth in Ohaffia consists mainly in land. Since access to this,
as we shall see later, is very largely through the mother's rights to
it, it is not surprising that where infant betrothal occurs, land and
the social status of the mates are important motives. But one must
at once admit that 'it is extremely difficult to determine the reasons
behind their choices'.[4] In the case of mature mates, where they can
choose for themselves, personal looks and personality traits would
also enter into their choice.

Absence of Widow-inheritance in Ohaffia

There are other features which seem to underline the strong
matrilineal bias of the Ohaffia system. Widow-inheritance, for
example, known and widely practised among the patrilineal Ibo,
is significantly absent among the Ohaffia Ibo. In a case discussed
in Chapter VII concerning the inheritance of private property in
Ohaffia, it is stated that Ego at his death left two widows behind.
About the fate of these widows, the court and the witnesses from
both sides of Ego's kin groups were emphatic: the women were
free not only to remarry if they wished but to marry whomsoever
they wanted, without interference from either Ego's matrilineage

---

[3] R. Needham, *Structure and Sentiment*, Chicago, Ill., 1962, p. 12 and
Chap. 3.
[4] Karlsson, 1963, p. 93.

or patrilineage. The Ohaffia, indeed, view widow-inheritance with horror, whereas among the patrilineal Ibo, it is a customary obligation of Ego's patrilineage to inherit the widow. In Ohaffia where a patrikin has no right to marry a kin's widow, there is also no obligation on him to care for her.

Divorce

Divorce in Ohaffia is usually granted merely at the wish of either spouse,[5] very much the opposite to patrilineal Ibo practice. It is of interest to note too that in patrilineal Ibo groups, the marriage payment is very much higher than in Ohaffia. In Ohaffia it rarely, until recently, exceeded a couple of pounds.[6] Among the patrilineal Ibo it may be as high as three hundred pounds. It has been suggested by some writers that where marriage payment is low, divorce is easy, and where high it is difficult.[7] Whether the differences in divorce practices and in the level of marriage payment have anything to do with matriliny or patriliny as Gluckman and others have suggested is another matter. There can be no simple explanation in causal terms. In Iboland today new factors have entered the situation. Parents now send their daughters to schools, colleges, and universities, or train them in career professions such as catering, nursing, and midwifery, and secretarial skills. This training is expensive and the cost is taken into account when girls are engaged to be married. They therefore account at least in part for the high marriage payments which now obtain among the patrilineal Ibo.[8] In Ohaffia too there is a marked increase[9] of payment made for marriage for precisely similar reasons. This, however, has not been comparable to the increase in some patrilineal Ibo communities, especially those of the Central Ibo whose marriage systems are, in Ardener's words, 'demand-sensitive'.[10]

[5] It is not being suggested here that ease of divorce means that its frequency is high, or that there is marital instability in Ohaffia.

[6] £1 to £2·50 was the range.

[7] M. Gluckman, 'Kinship and Marriage among the Lozi of Northern Rhodesia and the Zulu of Natal', in *African Systems of Kinship and Marriage*, ed. A. R. Radcliffe-Brown and D. Forde, London, 1950, pp. 166–206. See also E. Ardener, *Divorce and Fertility*, London, 1962, pp. 76–81.

[8] Cf. Ardener, 1962, pp. 76–7.

[9] The amount is between £15 and £20 now.

[10] Ardener, 1962, pp. 77–8. Here Ardener is arguing that 'in a society in which all men expect to marry . . .' the rise in the level of marriage payment 'is clearly bound up with rising prosperity'. In this case the 'marriage payment level' can be 'demand-sensitive'.

The Marriage of 'Purchased' Women in Ohaffia

Daughters are highly prized in Ohaffia, so much so that a prosperous Ohaffia household without any will endeavour to acquire or 'purchase' women from *outside* Ohaffia. This custom explains why a number of women who are not Ohaffia citizens by birth are found in big households in Ohaffia. They are 'purchased' mainly from the neighbouring patrilineal Ibibio and Ibo communities, as well as from groups east of Ohaffia at a much higher cost than Ohaffia women. When married they are referred to as either *àlùràlu* ('married' but also connoting 'purchased') or *Ohù nwanyì* ('slave woman'; 'slave' here connoting 'expensive').[11] The status assigned to such a wife is different (not 'inferior' but simply 'valuable') as compared to the status of a local wife.

It will be of interest to note in this connection that children resulting from such marriages, although regarded as full and free-born citizens, do not, by Ohaffia custom, belong to their father's patrilineage. On their father's death they are passed over to their father's matrilineage (*ikwu*) unless any of the children are old enough and of sufficient means to redeem their mother on her death by paying back to their father's matrilineage the price that Ohaffia custom prescribes. Payment, usually, is made in fixed quantities of livestock, drink, and clothes.

The Avunculate and Other Relationships in Ohaffia

The patterns of prescribed attitudes in the relations between (i) mother's brother and sister's son, (ii) father and son, (iii) brother and sister, and (iv) husband and wife in Ohaffia show a marked contrast with those between the same pairs of individuals among the patrilineal Ibo groups. I wish to discuss this contrast as it affects the patrilineal Ibo and the Ohaffia. I shall base the discussion on Lévi-Strauss's scheme which divides the attitudes involved in the relationships into two opposites: one positive, one negative. Under 'positive' are put all attitudes of familiarity, indulgence, and concern; and under 'negative', those attitudes reflecting unfamiliarity, concealed hostility, and respect. The positive is represented as 'plus' sign (+), and the negative as 'minus' sign (−). With this scheme as a basis I now proceed to

---

[11] As the Ohaffia do not pay that much for a local wife.

discuss these attitudes as far as I can guess them among the Ohaffia and the patrilineal Ibo.[12]

(i) *Mother's brother and sister's son.* In Ohaffia the relationship is one of unfamiliarity tinged with veiled mutual hostility. Sister's son stands in awe of mother's brother who under traditional circumstances exercises considerable authority over him. Sister's

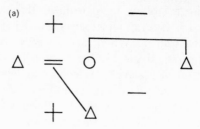

(a)

FIG. 8*a*. Ohaffia Ibo Pattern

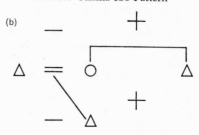

(b)

+ = Positive behaviour between each pair
− = Negative behaviour between each pair

FIG. 8*b*. 'Patrilineal' Ibo Pattern

son serves and obeys him in all matters. A similar pattern of attitudes also exists between mother's brother and his sister's daughter.

With the patrilineal Ibo, the pattern in this category of relationship is different. There it is one of extreme familiarity and indulgence.[13] Mother's brother has neither the power nor the rights which his counterpart in Ohaffia has over his sister's son (or daughter).

(ii) *Father and Son.* In Ohaffia the relationship is one of famili-

---

[12] I am aware that Lévi-Strauss's scheme is controversial in certain respects.

[13] There is a parallel here in the relationship between *Okele* (Ardener, 1954, p. 94) and mother's brother among the patrilineal *Ezinihite-Ibo*. See Green, 1947, p. 160.

arity and indulgence, and there is, I feel, some anxiety in the relationship on the part of the father over his son's future. In contrast, in the patrilineal Ibo pattern, authority is vested in the father who exercises it absolutely and sternly over his son.

(iii) *Brother and sister*. In Ohaffia this relationship seems to me to be one of unfamiliarity and uneasy aloofness. It contrasts again with the patrilineal Ibo pattern where brother and sister have close mutual respect towards each other.

(iv) *Husband and wife*. This relationship in Ohaffia seems to be one of mutual respect and accommodation of each other; it also seems to be positively harmonious. The contrary is the case among the patrilineal Ibo where the husband and wife relationship has a tinge of veiled hostility.

One could quite crudely sum up the four categories of relationships in the Ohaffia and in the patrilineal Ibo social systems as in Fig. 8. The 'plus' ($+$) and 'minus' ($-$) signs are my interpretations based on Lévi-Strauss's model. The Ohaffia pattern as represented is similar to that of the matrilineal Trobrianders[14] and if Lévi-Strauss is right it tends in a general sense to represent those of many matrilineal cultures.[15]

[14] C. Lévi-Strauss, *Structural Anthropology*, 1963, p. 45 (in his Charts).
[15] Ibid.

VII

INHERITANCE AND SUCCESSION IN OHAFFIA

As in other Ibo communities heritable property in Ohaffia is of two main categories: (i) land, fruit-trees, and dwellings, all of which can be referred to as immovable property; (ii) personal effects, clothes and ornaments, and other forms of goods and chattels such as utensils, furniture, and livestock, all of which can be described as movable property.

Again, the statuses to which an adult male or female may succeed in Ohaffia are of two categories: (i) sacred statuses such as the ritual headships of an extended family, and of a matrilineage; (ii) secular statuses, such as the headships of the secondary village division, *èzi*, of a matrilineage, or of a village. How the rights pertaining to these types of property and status are inherited in Ohaffia is the subject of this chapter.

I shall deal first with the rights to immovable property under the general heading of 'Rights to Land and its Resources', to be discussed under (*a*) patrilineal land rights, (*b*) matrilineal land rights, (*c*) village land rights, and (*d*) rights to private lands.

Rights to Land and its Resources

(*a*) *Patrilineal land rights.* As in other parts of Ibo country, residence in Ohaffia is patrilocal as a rule. Children grow in their father's kin group and reside in its territory permanently. Therefore the first kind of land right which adult male members of an Ohaffia patrilineage (*umudi*) should have is the right to the piece of village land upon which their dwellings stand: this piece of land is the building land (*èzi*). Rights to building land reside in the patrilineage as a group under the headship of the *Eze ezi* (the head of the patrilineally based 'secondary division' of the village, who in other parts of Ibo country will be called *Okpara*). Any adult male member of this can of right build on patrilineage land and live there permanently. If he dies without a son, any male member of his patrilineage—a brother, a brother's son, a half-sibling, or a half-sibling's son or a close patrikin member can take over the hut if it is still standing, or can build upon the vacant space. Where there are sons, the right passes to the eldest. This is the theory. In practice the occupation of a dead man's hut is never immediate; a period of time may elapse before permanent reoccupation can be effected. This is particularly true where ritual observances in honour of the deceased are waiting to be fulfilled. Sometimes, the hut is neglected and allowed to fall, particularly where the deceased left no heir, although in time any other male member of the patrilineage can build on the spot. Rights to patrilineal building land, therefore, are patrilineally inherited in Ohaffia as in patrilineal Ibo groups.

(b) *Matrilineal land rights.* The lands immediately beyond and adjoining the village building lands belong as a rule to the matrilineages in Ohaffia. Such lands are called *agbugbo ezi* (literally 'the bark of the residential land', i.e. the area surrounding it). Since members of a matrilineage (*ikwu*) in Ohaffia are dispersed, it follows that the matrilineage owning *agbugbo ezi* lands cannot live on these themselves. What generally happens is that the male (or female) head of the matrilineage owning such lands will take charge of them, however many and wherever these lands are. It is the responsibility of the head of the matrilineage to protect the rights of his matrilineage in such lands and the resources in or upon them, such as oil palms, raffia-palm groves, clay and chalk pits (*àlà uro* and *àlà nzu*). It is the responsibility of the male head of the matrilineage to supervise the use of these lands with the aid of the other adult members of the group.

I was told that about three-quarters of the *agbugbo ezi* land of Elu belongs to the matrilineage of Umu Aworo, under the care and supervision of the male head of the matrilineage named Uduma Odeghe. He himself belongs to the patrilineage (*umudi*) of Ndi Odeghe in the primary unit of Amaihe in Elu village. Another matrilineage, Umuezinkasi, I was told, owns the area of *agbugbo ezi* land between the local court and the new health centre in Ebem village. The head of this matrilineage, by name Okwun Eke, comes from a different village, Elu, and is of Ndiaja patrilineage (*umudi*) in Elu. The examples can be multiplied. It follows therefore that patrilineages (*umudi*) in Ohaffia sometimes settle or do their farming on lands pledged from matrilineages (*ikwu*). When such sites become abandoned[1] they revert to the matrilineages from whom the sites were originally pledged. Where also *agbugbọ ezi* land used as farmland becomes abandoned, this reverts to the owning matrilineage.

(c) *Village land rights*. Lands lying sometimes many miles away, beyond *agbugbọ ezi*, are generally also owned by matrilineages. But sometimes, though very rarely, such lands can be owned by a whole village, especially if they are frontier lands. Frontier lands of this kind are called *agu ukwu* (big bush), and if owned by one village are also significantly called *nkpakọ* (common land). Otherwise a whole village rarely possesses land as a village. A known example of such village-owned land is that claimed by the village of Amaekpu. It lies some six miles on the ridge highway north-west of Ohaffia on the boundary between Amaekpu and Okagwe. Ohaffia people farm in blocks of farmland continuously stretching for a mile or more. Farmlands are marked out during each farming season under the supervision of the elders (*ndi ichin*) of the owning village and allotted to the various patrilineages comprising the village.

But because most lands belong to matrilineages in Ohaffia, patrilineages are generally compelled to pledge lands from matrilineages. The lands so pledged are called *àlà ukwuzì* (literally 'lands under a pledge'). But because a man inherits rights to land through his matrilineage, and because matrilineally owned lands are scattered, a man can therefore have more than one farm at a time worked by him with the help of his wives and of his matrilineally related female kin.

(d) *Rights to private lands*. Lands purchased or otherwise acquired by an individual are private lands. At the owner's death, provided the lands are not built on, such lands will be inherited by the appropriate member of the deceased's matrilineage, usually a sister's son, or in the absence of one by the closest male or female member of the man's matrilineage. A known case is discussed later in connection with rights to movable property. The contrary is the case in patrilineal Ibo groups where, at the death of the owner, lands of this sort go to his male children,[2] with the eldest son inheriting the chief share, or in the absence of a son, to

---

[1] In Ohaffia abandoned settlement sites are called *okpùrukpu*.

[2] In the manner set out by M. M. Green in her *Land Tenure in an Ibo Village*, London, 1941, pp. 12–13.

a brother, or to the closest patrikin. In Ohaffia the man's children will have no rights to such lands, nor would any of his close patrikin. Because of the way in which private lands are inherited in Ohaffia, lands owned by matrilineages there have a much greater tendency to multiply than those owned by patrilineage groups.

As a matter of fact an Ohaffia man would rather get a member of his own matrilineage to buy a piece of land which he himself cannot afford to buy than let a member of his own patrilineage do so. He is in fact expected by custom to do this. This is why matrilineal lands are generally acquired in bits and pieces all the time and why such lands lie scattered over a wide area. But they permanently remain within the matrilineage passing on whenever possible from one male to another in the female line.

The pattern of landownership for the three categories of people so far discussed shows three concentric circles of land types: the innermost being the village building-land occupied by village primary units (further subdivided by the secondary ones within each primary). This innermost circle, as we have earlier observed, is the *èzi*. Then the next outer circle is unbuilt-on land owned by matrilineages, whose members are dispersed. This circle of land is the *agbugbọ ezi* as already noted. Thirdly come lands the owners of which may be mixed, including the village as a whole, matrilineages, as well as private individuals. These are *ágù* bush or lands. An Ohaffia man through this system receives three kinds of land rights: patrilineal, matrilineal, and personal or private rights.

With regard to resources on or in the land, such as food-trees, or clay and chalk-pits, all these are communally owned and exploited by the groups owning the lands where they grow, or are found, or by the person who planted them, and are inherited either matrilineally or patrilineally according to where the ownership of the lands carrying them lies. Wild or semi-wild crops, such as oil palm, and leaves used as vegetables, or timber used for building, and other wild plant products are freely exploited by those who can.

Rights to Movable or Personally Acquired Property

I have indicated earlier what movable property may consist of. This has greatly multiplied today and may, apart from furniture and cooking utensils, include radio, radiogram, bicycle, sewing machine, and possibly a motor-car. Personally acquired property nowadays usually consists of lands which have been purchased outright.[3] When a man dies within Ohaffia and not outside it, laying claim to his movable property by his sister's son or by the closest matrilineal male or female kin presents no problem at all even in a case of an unexpected death. Custom requires that such movable property should be passed on in the maternal line. The man's physical and spiritual well-being is the direct responsibility of his matrilineage, and so is the cost of his burial at death.

But problems arise sometimes if a man's death occurs outside Ohaffia. In this case it is the responsibility of the special courts set up by the Regional Judiciary, to determine, according to Ohaffia custom, the claims of persons who seek the courts' certification of their right to inherit the property of relatives whose deaths have occurred outside Ohaffia. The special courts' proceedings follow definite terms of reference given by the Divisional Officer in charge of the Bende Division in a letter,[4] and the courts go through all the formalities which the ordinary law-court would follow in a civil dispute. The prospective inheritor will be required to lodge his claim at the office of the Divisional Officer. A date is fixed for the hearing, witnesses are called from both the patrilineal and the maternal kin of the deceased. A panel of judges with one of them as president and a court clerk sit to record their findings and to pronounce verdict. The action is not seen as a dispute as this is understood in law. But the court's action is necessary so that the rightful claimant can be provided with a legal document which will enable him to exercise his customary rights over the deceased relative's property outside Ohaffia where the custom regarding inheritance may be different.

We can now follow an actual case of a claim of this sort from Fig. 9, which is discussed as follows: Ego died in Umuahia township outside Ohaffia in 1964, leaving behind both landed property and movable property, as well as two wives (nos. 3 and 7 in Fig. 9), and eight children ('a' to 'h'). Ego had a maternal uncle (no. 1) but no sister's son, because he had no sister. Ego also had

---

[3] Among the patrilineal Ibo, sale of land is impossible. In Ohaffia land is sold. This is particularly true of lands other than *ezi* and *agbugbŏ ezi*.

[4] The letter would simply request that 'A Judicial Inquiry be set up to determine the next of kin in respect of X (the deceased) as to who should inherit and administer the afore-named deceased estates in accordance with Ohaffia Native Law and Custom of Inheritance', Record Book, No. 4/60, District Court Grade A, Ebem, Ohaffia, 1965.

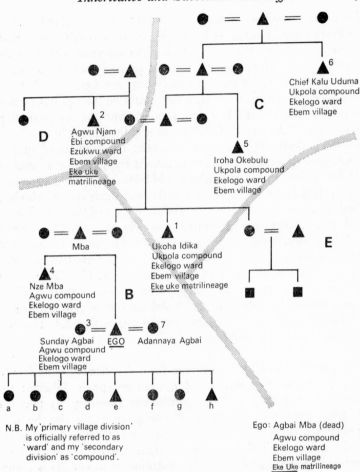

FIG. 9. The Genealogical Links of Witnesses in the case described in the text

a maternal grand-uncle (no. 2), a male half-sibling (no. 4), and two other maternal kin (nos. 5 and 6). The person who in the absence of a sister's son is the closest maternal kin who can lay a legitimate claim to Ego's movable property and landed estate in the township is his mother's brother (no. 1). The court's decision about this was unanimous. The maternal uncle was declared the rightful person to whom all Ego's property, according to Ohaffia custom, should go. The six witnesses called (nos. 1 to 6), who included Ego's male half-sibling (no. 4), testified to this too. The court also ruled that the responsibility of paying Ego's debts, if any, and of bringing up Ego's eight children as he would his own children was that of no. 1. To this judgement, which was concerned with the rule governing the inheritance of personal property, corollaries were stated: (i) if it had been Ego's uncle and not Ego who died, by Ohaffia custom Ego as a sister's son would be the rightful person to inherit his mother's brother's property and the corresponding obligations; (ii) if Ego had been a minor at the time of his mother's brother's death, by the same principle, Ego's maternal grand-uncle (no. 2) would have had to inherit the property as well as the obligations of the man who would be to him a sister's son (i.e. no. 1). If it had been Ego's maternal grand-uncle (no. 2) who had died, then no. 1, a sister's son, would be the rightful inheritor.

It can be seen from Fig. 9 that those who are linked by the rule of inheritance, namely Ego, his maternal uncle (no. 1), his maternal grand-uncle (no. 2), belong to the same matrilineage (*ikwu*), which bears in this case the name of the ancestress Eke Uke. These three comprised a property-inheriting group to which their children could belong. It will be of incidental interest to note that Ego's senior wife came from the same patrilineage as Ego did. This was the Ndi Agwu secondary unit.

Three firm conclusions emerge from the discussion so far: (i) that there are two recognized descent-groups in Ohaffia: the matrilineage (*ikwu*) and the patrilineage (*umudi*); (ii) that the matrilineage is not only the exogamous group but is also the main property-inheriting and landowning group in Ohaffia. Its members claim common allegiance from the ancestress by whose name the group is called; and (iii) that the patrilineage in Ohaffia is a non-exogamous group, and it can only inherit certain categories of land. The patrilineage is, however, the residential group, its members also laying claim to a common ancestor.

This system of descent will be discussed further. All that we have said so far about the Ohaffia concerning their rules of in-heritance is reversed among the patrilineal Ibo groups. There the patrilineage (*umu nna*) is the exogamous group, and sometimes even villages stand in the same strict exogamous relationship with one another.[5] In these other Ibo communities, the patrilineage is also the property-inheriting group.

[5] Meek, 1937, p. 259; Green, 1947, pp. 149–59; Ardener, 1959, pp. 128–9.

The Headship of the Matrilineage

An Ohaffia matrilineage has two heads, one generally male, one always female. Each status moves to each new successor in the patrilineage in which he or she permanently resides. The existence of two heads arises from the kind of duties devolving on the incumbents. These duties are of two categories: (*a*) secular, (*b*) sacred.

(*a*) *Secular duties.* These are the responsibility of the male. It is he who settles disputes among members of his matrilineage. But his more important duties are the protection of the rights and interests of members in the lands or estates and the resources of these; he appoints those who apportion matrilineal lands to members and others who need to use them over a period; it is he who permits the exploitation of plant and soil resources from their common estates, and protects these against abuse or selfish use. He takes court action against trespassers or usurpers. It is he who would permit the pledging of parts of the estates but with the knowledge and consent of his matrilineage. He keeps count of the estates, and keeps alive the histories of how the lands and their plant-resources were acquired.[6] He sees to their increase and endeavours in his lifetime to add to them. When no males are available or if they are still minors, an adult female can head the matrilineage.

(*b*) *Sacred duties.* These are the responsibility of the female head of a matrilineage and are mainly of ritual character. It is the female head (*Ezè nwanyi*) who makes sacrifices to the sacred pots (*ùdùdù*) each of which represents an ancestress, both on specific occasions prescribed by custom or at an emergency following the request for such a rite by the member of the matrilineage whose well-being needs to be assured. A male cannot be its ritual head. The status is succeeded to matrilineally and by lineage seniority. The cult of the ancestress is discussed more fully in Chapter IX.

True as it is that the deepest feeling of warmth and welcome awaits the Ibo man in his mother's brother's household, it is even more so for an Ohaffia Ibo. An Ohaffia person makes a great deal of fuss about 'those with whom I share the same womb' (*otù afọ*). The people are open about their strong bias towards their mothers

---

[6] An example of a history of this sort but relating to the patrilineage of Ndi Ukwa and showing lands owned, pledged, or lost is to be found in the Appendix.

and mothers' own kin group. They affirm this in proverbs, jests, and jibes: 'we eat through mother' (*ayi neli nà nne*). Or if, for instance, members of a matrilineage meeting as a group were taunted by a passer-by and jokingly accused of conspiring against their patrikin, the quick retort would be: 'Yes, but don't you hear the Ohaffia say that a man's worst enemy is his patrikin (*umudi bù agha*)?' Sometimes the retort is the jibe 'Yes, father's penis scatters, mother's womb gathers' (*utù* = 'penis', *natusa atusa* = 'scatters'; *ikpù* = 'womb', *n'ekpokota ekpokota* = 'gathers'). There are numerous other ways in which this verbal moat built around their 'matrilineal' castle can be as effectively used as has just been indicated. Although, as a rule, members of an Ohaffia matrilineage are territorially dispersed, their allegiance to both the living heads of the group and the sacred pots (*ùdùdù*) of their ancestresses, with the strict imposition of matrilineage exogamy, give them the formidable degree of cohesion which the lack of a common residential base does not at all weaken or diminish.

VIII

SUCCESSION TO VILLAGE HEADSHIP

Rules of Succession[1]

NO general rule of succession applies in Ohaffia for the selection of *Eze ogo*, the village head. Nor is the rule adopted by one village or a group of them always strictly observed. This is partly because wealth and influence sometimes govern a choice.[2] For the general Ibo, the position is different. It is possible to say that they follow a general rule in selecting the village *okpara*.[3]

This absence of a general rule in Ohaffia can be seen from Table 2, where as many as nine different rules apply. The two villages in Group (*a*), Elu and Ihenta, have alternate succession: a rule by which the oldest free-born male from either of two 'tertiary' patrilineages in the senior 'primary' village division of Elu, or from either of the two 'primary' patrilineages in Ihenta succeeds to the headship of that village in turn. Ihenta is a small village, comprising two 'primaries' only. In this case, both 'secondary' and 'tertiary' units are absent. It is difficult to argue that its small size bears any relation to the rule of succession it has adopted. In Group (*b*), for example, there are at least four small villages: Amuma, Ndi Okala, Ndi Amogu, and Ndi Uduma Ukwu, which seem to follow the general Ibo principle which confers the village headship upon the senior male of the senior 'tertiary' patrilineage of the senior 'secondary' patrilineage group.

In Elu, Group (*a*), usurpation is given as the explanation for the rule of alternate succession followed there. In this case, where an explanation is available, we shall take the opportunity later to

---

[1] The material used in this chapter was not collected by me in the field but from official records in the National Archives of Eastern Nigeria. See Official Communications: No. 10411/12 of January 1934, and No. 29196 of 13 March 1934.

[2] That wealth and influence play an important part was also recognized by British administration officials in the early thirties. See Official Communications, loc. cit.

[3] Meek, 1937, p. 109.

TABLE 2. *The Rules of Succession to Village Headship in Ohaffia*

Group	Name of Village		Rule of Succession
(a)	1. Elu 2. Ihenta		Alternate succession: the oldest free-born male of two 'tertiary' patrilineages; neither is the senior 'tertiary' of the founder of the village.
(b)	1. Akanu 2. Ndi Ibe 3. Amangwu 4. Amuma 5. Ufiele	6. Ndi Okala 7. Ndi Amogu 8. Ndi Anku 9. Ndi Uduma Ukwu 10. Nkwebi	The oldest free-born male of the senior 'tertiary' patrilineage of the senior 'secondary' village unit.
c)	1. Amaekpu 2. Eziafo		The oldest free-born male of a 'tertiary' patrilineage, but not the senior 'tertiary', of the senior 'secondary' village unit.
d)	1. Amuke		The oldest free-born from any of the five 'secondary' village units.
(e)	1. Okonu 2. Abia 3. Okagwe		The oldest male from a 'tertiary' patrilineage, but not the senior 'tertiary', of the founder of the village.
(f)	1. Isi Ugwu		The oldest male from two 'tertiary' patrilineages of the senior 'secondary' village unit.
(g)	1. Asaga 2. Oboro	3. Ndi Uduma- Awoke	Not determined.
(h)	1. Ndi Orieke		The senior 'tertiary' patrilineage of the second senior 'secondary' village unit.
(i)	1. Ebem		Matrilineal succession. The oldest male survivor descended matrilineally from Eke Uke, the second daughter of Chiasara the ancestress and founder of Ebem village.

discuss the implications of the event at Elu from the standpoint of the general Ibo kinship ideology. In Group (*b*), as already noted, the ten villages follow a different principle from the two villages in Group (*a*); this appears to correspond with the general rule of succession among the 'patrilineal' Ibo.

In Group (*c*) there is again reason to suspect usurpation as in Elu. Here the two villages choose their head from a 'tertiary' patrilineage group which in neither case is the senior 'tertiary' patrilineage of the senior 'secondary' patrilineage group. The one

village in Group (*d*) follows a rule which again is completely different from any so far discussed. In this village, any free-born male
from any of the five 'secondary' patrilineage groups, provided he
is the oldest, may become the village head. The factor of seniority
of the 'tertiary' patrilineages does not seem to be an important
enough consideration. This village is also small although it is
difficult, as noted earlier, to see that size is a factor. In Group (*e*)
usurpation also seems to have occurred as in Group (*a*) and probably as in Group (*c*), for in Group (*e*) the only 'tertiary' patrilineage
which provides the village head is not the senior patrilineage of the
village founder's 'secondary' group.

In Group (*f*) the rule of alternate succession as in Group (*a*)
recurs, and disagreement rather than usurpation seems to be indicated. In Group (*g*) the position is undetermined. It is of interest
to note that it is in this group that we have at present one of the
most serious disputes over village headship in Ohaffia. The in-
determinate state of affairs over such an important status is very
much unlike the Ibo, where 'the order of seniority of the various
branches of the kindred is usually well recognized . . .'[4] In Group
(*h*), in which there is only one village, usurpation also appears to
have taken place. Here it is the senior 'tertiary' patrilineage of the
second senior 'secondary' group that provides the village head.

In the last group, Group (*i*), in which there is again one village,
Ebem, the matrilineal principle is seen to be operative. Here it is
the oldest male survivor[5] matrilineally descended from the second
daughter, Eke Uke, of the village ancestress (*chiasara*) who
succeeds to the village headship.

Such is the variety of rules of succession to village headship in
Ohaffia. We observed earlier that this state of affairs is uncharacter-
istic of the Ibo. It is difficult to find a satisfactory explanation for
the anomaly, that is, if viewed from the standpoint of the strict rule
of seniority which regulates succession to all kinds of headships
among the 'patrilineal' Ibo groups, be these the headships of the
'tertiary' patrilineages, or of the 'secondary' ones, or even of the
village, or the village group. The stress on character and attain-
ments in Ohaffia rather than on the seniority of age and lineage is
significant. If one is tempted to explain their 'system' of succession

[4] Meek, 1937, pp. 108–9.
[5] Chief Kalu Uduma, No. 6 in Fig. 9 is the present village head (*Eze ogo*) of
Ebem. His mother, incidentally, is the head of the matrilineage.

as an attempt to ensure effective leadership and thereby ensure as well the survival of the group in a hostile frontier environment, this would not explain the intrusive factors of wealth and influence which are not often compatible with the ability to lead.

At the extended family[6] level in Ohaffia where succession follows the 'patrilineal' Ibo principle, no cases of usurpation were admitted. As in other Ibo groups, the head of the extended family is called *Okpara*, although those of the 'tertiary' and the 'secondary' patrilineage groups are called *Eze ezi*, and that of a village, *Eze ogo*, not *Okpara* as in 'patrilineal' Ibo groups. This difference in the terms used would support my theory that *Eze ezi* and *Eze ogo* are semi-titular statuses,[7] which are achieved, not ascribed as *Okpara*-ship is. The facts as we know them today regarding the choice of the village head give the impression that the right of succession resides in lineage groups although selection would tend, as we have seen, to be influenced by the factors of wealth and personal qualities.

We said before that succession to the headship of an Ohaffia matrilineage takes two forms because of the difference in the kind of responsibilities associated with this status in a matrilineage. There is therefore no conflict between matrilineal rule of succession and succession by patrilineal rule. In each case the responsibilities are different, but the two rules produce two exclusive systems of succession in Ohaffia.

Ibo Kinship Ideology and Succession in Ohaffia

The different forms which succession to Ohaffia village headship takes seem to lay the 'system' open to disputes and to usurpatory acts. I shall briefly examine in this section the social implications of such acts in terms of the ideology of Ibo kinship. The case of usurpation generally stated to have occurred at Elu where the *Eze ogo* (village head) is no longer supplied by the true 'tertiary' patrilineage group[8] of the village, but curiously enough[9]

---

[6] This will be a 'fourth division' patrilineage group.

[7] Titles, such as *Ozó* and *Eze* are largely acquired through wealth, although those like *Onowu* and *Isagba* are heritable in the group, but the choice of a candidate may sometimes be affected by wealth and influence. See Meek, 1937, on 'Titles', Chapter VII and on 'Kinship', Chapter VIII.

[8] The name of the patrilineage is *Ndi Imagha Uwa*.

[9] The names of the two junior patrilineages are *Umu Okoro-azu* and *Umu Anya*.

by two junior tertiary patrilineage groups,[10] will provide the basis for this brief examination.

What happened at Elu was said to be as follows: at a certain time in the history of the village, the senior partilineage (it was alleged) committed a ritual offence against the two other units of the 'secondary' patrilineage group by paying the traditional homage to the ancestral mother in preference to the ancestral father of the group. For this offence the right of the senior patrilineage as head of Elu was usurped.

The interesting point about the incident is that what the three patrilineages involved in the conflict did was in direct opposition to the kinship ideology of the 'patrilineal' Ibo. Not only would homage to an ancestral mother in preference to the ancestral father be unusual; no junior patrilineage, whatever the pretext, would usurp the right or the status of its senior patrilineage with whom consanguinity was claimed. And in no 'patrilineal' Ibo community would two related patrilineages jointly own and exercise the right to a village headship, even if the right were exercised in rotation as at Elu. That usurpation would normally not occur or be contemplated in a 'patrilineal' Ibo group particularly where consanguinity is believed to exist, is explained by the fact that rules of succession to a patrilineage, or to a village headship (*Okpara*) in an Ibo community are usually indisputably clear and strictly adhered to, and are regulated on the basis of lineage seniority.[11] The rules are sustained by supernatural sanctions of the kind that the Ibo on the whole profoundly dread. Their belief is that violent death would overtake the usurping lineage, a death which they say 'uproots the lineage' (*honi mbànà*).[12]

The ideology of Ibo kinship also implies that seniority can only be claimed by one lineage at a time. This would normally rule out the possibility of competing claims. Moreover a senior lineage retains its right to its status in perpetuity, as long as the lineage members of the group continue to acknowledge and recognize a common ancestry and the ideology which this implies. That is the position both in theory and in practice among the 'patrilineal' Ibo.

It is of course true that a new group settling among an older

---

[10] In 1934 R. O. Ramage, British administrative official, reported that 'it was a curious fact that the senior true family in Elu does not supply the Eze ogo'. See the Memorandum to the Secretary Southern Provinces dated 15 May 1934 (by R. O. Ramage), National Archives, Enugu, Eastern Nigeria.

[11] Meek, 1937, p. 109.

[12] Ibid., p. 108.

group would remain a political threat to it. But once the new group has been adopted into the older group, the ideology would become applicable and binding to the group so adopted.[13] Thus the possibility of usurpation would be contained, or at least greatly diminished.

With the position as outlined, the sort of usurpation alleged at Elu can now be seen to be irregular in terms of the ideology of Ibo kinship. For the same reason the right of succession to a village headship in a 'patrilineal' Ibo community can neither be jointly owned nor jointly exercised even in rotation by two or more lineages as is now happening at Elu. Similarly, because of the patrilineal basis of this ideology one can now see why it is unlikely that a 'patrilineal' Ibo group would do homage to an ancestress rather than to an ancestor.

In view of all this, a more acceptable explanation for the series of 'irregular' acts alleged at Elu would have to be sought. A plausible one would be that the three lineages could not have had a common genealogical ancestry. If they did, the usurpation, by the rules of the kinship ideology of the Ibo, would not have occurred. If the lineages had a 'patrilineal' basis only, the senior lineage would not have paid homage to an ancestress.

The initial recognition of one lineage as the senior by the two other lineages, assuming that the three had no common genealogical ancestry, can be explained by the fact that such recognition is usually given if the 'senior' lineage was the first to settle at the village site before the other two joined in later.[14] It is quite possible that there was some distant kinship link between the 'senior' lineage and the other two for the latter to be able to join with the former initially, although it need not be so in each case. But the more distant the kinship bond, the weaker it tends to become. There would come a time when this bond would be too weak to deter any usurpatory act or to prevent the two lineages from pulling out of their original commitment in recognizing the first lineage as their senior. Once this first step towards withdrawal of recognition began, the next logical act would be usurpation under whatever pretext.

Moreover, we know that the Ohaffia have traditions which speak of 'waves' of their own kin joining with earlier groups, and sometimes even with 'stranger' groups. We also know that in Elu,

[13] Meek, 1937, p. 109.   [14] Ibid.

the two lineages now jointly holding the headship of Elu outnumber the 'senior' lineages. The latter in fact seem on the verge of
demise. The agreement to keep the headship in joint ownership
can be explained as a compromise decision by the two 'junior'
lineages in order to avoid future conflict between themselves.

An alternative explanation for the 'irregularities' we speak of
would be that what occurred at Elu was due to contact with
the Ekoid-speaking communities east and south-east of Ohaffia
country. The 'irregularities' therefore might be 'borrowed' cultural
traits. That this explanation might well be the more acceptable one
we shall later try to show. But there can be little doubt that the
absence of one generally accepted rule of succession to village
headships in Ohaffia is largely responsible for the constant disputes
over these. The current dispute at Asaga which has been long-
standing provides an example.

IX

THE DEAD AMONG THE LIVING
IN OHAFFIA

Ancestral Monuments

THE Ibo believe that their dead live on, that they continue to take active interest in the affairs of their living descendants.[1] The cult of ancestors and the custom of representing ancestors in clay and wooden symbols which the Ibo have, rest upon this belief. However, while among the patrilineal Ibo female ancestors are not represented,[2] in Ohaffia both male and female ancestors are. This contrast is significant.

Ancestral symbols are very much in evidence in Ohaffia, and on the whole are well preserved.[3] This is unlike some parts of Iboland where, partly as a result of the spread of Christianity, neglect has caused considerable decrease in their numbers. The churches too have actively encouraged and on occasions participated in the mass destruction of these objects. Ohaffia therefore provides a rare exception. The Church of Scotland Mission, which still has the dominant influence in Ohaffia, is said to have taken a more tolerant view of the 'heathen' beliefs and practices from the start, and did not engage in active destruction of cult objects.[4] Ohaffia has also escaped the excesses of syncretistic sects whose own brands of evangelism also too often erupt into public displays of mass destruction of fetishes and ancestral objects.

In the present chapter we shall be dealing with ancestral monuments only, as they are still to be found in Ohaffia today. They fall into two main types, one consists of natural objects, such

[1] Meek, 1937, p. 66. [2] Ibid., p. 62.

[3] The Nigerian Dept. of Antiquities has in recent years been actively engaged in promoting the preservation *in situ* of fetishes as well as ancestral objects in Ohaffia.

[4] The Revd. Fr. O'Kieve of the Roman Catholic Mission in Enugu Ngwo periodically carried out religious campaigns of mass destruction by burning of cult objects in various parts of Iboland east of the Niger. In 1962 I travelled to parts of Mbaise and Nekede in Owerri Province to try to stop the burning and to save what I could for the Department of Antiquities.

as a rock outcrop, or a piece of log, that have come to be associated with the founders of local groups. The other type comprises man-made monuments, such as an *òbu* or an *ùdùdù* (pot). The two types are discussed below.

Type 1. A well-known example in this group is a log which can still be seen in the rest-hut (*òbu*) of the Ndi Ofali, in Amaekpu village. The log is said to be of a 'timeless' origin and described by the owning group as *osisi anamagh onye butere ya* ('a tree which no one knows who brought it'). Ofali, the founder of the 'secondary' village unit which bears his name, is believed to have found the log in the form that it still is, and on the spot where he subsequently settled and erected his hut. The living members of Ndi Ofali treat the log as an ancestral monument and regard it as representing Ofali himself. They treat the log with great reverence. During my first visit to Ndi Ofali in 1961 the log was left in the open, where it was supposed to have been found originally by Ofali. It then rested on two wooden posts. It has now been moved into the Ndi Ofali rest-hut (*òbu*).

The rock outcrop in the village of Amuma is in the same category as the Ndi Ofali log. The rock has imprints which are believed to be the footprints of 'a powerful race of dwarfs', *òha odù* ('people with tail'), who were believed to have stood upon the rock and dented it with their tread. The rock is about a mile outside the village, and has been adopted by the village community of Amuma as their ancestral symbol representing the founder of the village who is said to be a female.

Type 2. The monuments in this group are man-made. They sometimes represent a founding ancestor who is often described as a warrior or as a hunter, or they may represent any member in a line of ancestors. Where they represent the founders of patri-lineage groups, the monuments take the form of *òbu* (rest-huts). The monuments in this category are far more numerous than those in Type 1. Those in Type 1 are owned by 'secondary' patrilineage groups or even villages. Thus as one descends from the village founder to ancestors of village segments, ancestral monuments become more and more numerous in Ohaffia. Thus, whereas an Ohaffia village may have one ancestral monument representing the founder of that village, it can also have numerous other monuments representing the founding ancestors of village segments. This explains why each 'secondary' village unit has its

own *òbu* built for its own founder, and why there are as many *òbu*
as there are secondary village units in Ohaffia. On the other hand,
pots are used to represent the numerous individual ancestors, male
and female, who make up individual
lineages, one pot raised for one
ancestor.

Height 126 in.

FIG. 10. Ohaffia Post. Posts
like this are seen to carry the
beams of *Òbu*.

It is significant that 'primary'
village units have no ancestral
monuments, but villages and lineages
have. The *òbu* monument of Ndi
Edike 'secondary' unit in Mgbaga
and 'secondary' village units in Ebem
village, is described here. Like all
others, its structure and ground-plan
are simple. It is oblong in shape,
about 50 feet long and half that
length in width, and it stands up to
18 feet high, from the ridge of the
roof to the floor. Three upright posts
support the ridge. Each post is
ornately carved and centrally posi-
tioned on the long axis of the *òbu* to
display in full view the carved symbols on it. The symbols, which as
a rule consist of stylized pots or
stools carried on human or animal
heads, are worked in relief. The
human heads are said to be those of
slaves or captives in war (Fig. 10). It
is significant that in Ohaffia tradi-
tional war-dances, pots (though generally described as human
skulls) are carried by dancers on the head in a manner similar
to the symbols described here.[5]

Most *òbu*, like the one we are describing here, have three
rooms of unequal sizes, the largest room lying between the two
small ones (Fig. 11). This large room is the meeting-hall where
the elders of the Ndi Edike, the owning 'secondary' patrilineage group, meet. High mud-benches (in certain other *òbu*,

[5] To carry an object on the head in an Ibo ceremony is to display its worth.
One may assume that the Ohaffia do this for the same reason.

modern wooden ones) are seen to line only three sides of the meeting-hall.

It is in Room 2 (Fig. 11), one of the two smaller rooms, that the pot monuments of the male ancestors of Ndi Edike are stored, away from public view. The transfer of the male pots from the pot huts of the different 'tertiary' patrilineage groups is a recent development. Unauthorized entry into the small room where the male ancestral pots are now stored is forbidden.

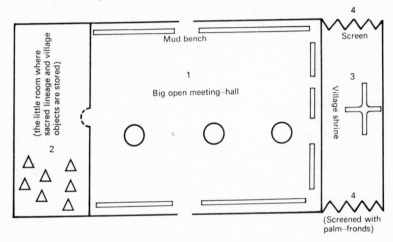

FIG. 11. Ground-Plan of *Òbu*, Ebem Village

The other small room (No. 3, Fig. 11) is open at two ends marked (4) in the figure, but these are discreetly screened with young palm-fronds to prevent the undue exposure to public view of the shrine housed in it. The shrine is that of the tutelary spirit, the *Òbu Nkwa*, of the Ndi Edike. Much of the prestige and respect enjoyed by this patrilineage rests upon the alleged power of this spirit. Again, unauthorized entry into the shrine or the room in which it is housed is strictly barred.

We have said before that each 'secondary' village unit in Ohaffia has its own *òbu* in which its male ancestral pots are now stored. But not every *òbu* in Ohaffia houses the tutelary spirit of its owners. In every case, however, the big room is the meeting-hall. Thus, the *òbu* can be seen to serve two social functions, one sacred, one secular. But no one sleeps in it, although men may drink in it. In the village of Amuma, I observed a competitive drinking contest at an annual ritual ceremony going on in the *òbu*, but no eating was seen to have taken place.

The *Òbu Nkwa* of Ndi Ezera in Asaga village seems to have a unique function for Ohaffia as a whole. It is said that it was the only one in Ohaffia to which anyone in danger could be assured *ukwuzi* ('shelter'). Unlike most *òbu*, it has no meeting-hall; the whole of it is taken up by massive male and female figures carved in wood. The male figures, in sitting posture, rest their hands on their knees, their feet upon the carved figures of slaves. The females, also sitting, carry babes in their arms and the *Òbu Nkwa* itself is barred to unauthorized entry. No black material or head-gear may be worn on entry, and one must enter on bare feet and in the company of the *Ezè Òbu* (the *òbu* priest). The Asaga *Òbu Nkwa*, as it is now generally known, is certainly the best known outside Ohaffia, and has since been declared a national monument by the Federal Government.

Now compared with what might be regarded as its equivalent among the patrilineal Ibo groups, where such rest-huts are variously called *òbi*, *òvu*, *obiriama*,[6] an Ohaffia *òbu*, particularly in terms of function, contrasts with those of the general Ibo. Among the riverain Ibo, for example (Abo, Asaba, and Onitsha Ibo) the *òbi* there is lived in by the *opara uku* ('big elder') of the owning village unit or the *opara nta* ('small elder') of a smaller lineage segment. Because of this additional residential function, the house-plan is such that the living-rooms are arranged behind the front open hall which, in fact, is the *òbi*. It is in the *òbi* that the elders meet, drink, rest, and gossip. Ancestor-cult objects such as clay or carved wooden figures (for example, *Ikengà*), or the skulls or the jaw-bones of goats sacrificed to ancestors, are stood on or hung over a raised mud platform on the front part of the *òbi*. The *òbi*, therefore, serve the multiple function of a home, an an-cestral shrine, and a meeting-place in the parts of Iboland where they exist.

There are a few other structural differences of detail between the Ohaffia *òbu* and the *òbi* of the general Ibo. The mud bench, which is the shrine, where ancestral cult-objects are, is at the open end of the *òbi* and in full view. The mud benches which line the three walls of the *òbi* are so constructed as to reflect distinctions of status. The bench on which the elder sits or lies is higher and

---

[6] Meek calls them 'entrance huts', 1937, p. 62.

bigger than the others. It has a raised mud head-rest and lies against the longest wall facing the cult-objects, and overlooking the open courtyard. No one else lower in rank may sit on it, although children do, and males whose mothers come from the patrilineage group also may.[7]

In Ohaffia these distinctions are not made. The *òbu* mud-benches there are of uniform size, although the *eze òbu* (*òbu* priest) is accorded the privilege of choosing his seat first in the *òbu*. It illustrates an aspect of the Ibo way of thinking which, although aware of status and rank, also recognizes at the same time the equality of claims to certain basic rights which any free-born Ibo citizen should enjoy. Thus an Ohaffia elder may be accorded such courtesies as the offer of a seat, drink, or kola, first, without the implication of superior birth or blood. It is not the custom in Ohaffia, or in any other Ibo group for that matter, to rank a free-born by the criterion of privileged birth except where there is a tradition of kingship. Similar thinking applies to the use of a position of authority among the Ibo.[8]

Male Ancestral Pots

We noted that pots are raised to male and female ancestors in Ohaffia. Male ancestral pots are in the charge of patrilineages (*umudi*), whereas female ancestral pots are kept and cared for by the female members of a matrilineage (*ikwu*).

We shall discuss male pots first. These accumulate in this manner. A son is required by custom, some time after his father's death, to raise a pot to his father's memory, just as his father

---

[7] This is one of a number of privileges which a man is entitled to in his matrilineage, *ndi nne*, or *umunne*, where he enjoys extraordinary freedom from control. He is variously referred to in different parts of Iboland as *okele*, or *nwa nwa* (Ardener, 1954, pp. 97, 98), *nwa ọkpu* ('child of anus'), *nwa aji* ('child of pubic hair').

[8] An interesting incident which illustrates the point about Ibo distrust of absolute authority was noted by O. W. Firth, the Senior Resident, Owerri Province, in his comments on a report by L. T. Chubb, a junior administrative officer, on an Ibo 'clan'. Chubb reported an Ibo elder, Ndubuwa by name, as saying: 'I am head of the head village in Ibere and I am expected to do the talking but anything I say has been agreed to by all of us and I do not want Government to exalt me above others. It is not our custom and we distrust it.' Commenting on this statement, Firth minuted: 'In my view this statement of Ndubuwa correctly represents true native custom on the subject and is evidence that it is a mistake in an Ibo country to invest an individual with authority which is not his by custom' (see Resident's Covering Report, No. OW. 1087/36 of 28 Apr. 1933, National Archives, Enugu).

should have done for his own father, and so on, going up the male ancestral line. One can still see on the paths in village 'primaries' huts containing some of these patrilineage pots. As pots are traditionally permanently housed on a spot of patrilineage ground, the number of pot grounds in a given secondary lineage group should in theory correspond to the number of smaller lineage segments which make up the group. But this hardly happens in practice. Sometimes pot grounds outnumber patrilineage segments, and sometimes segments outnumber pot grounds. It is easy to see how either could have happened. Where there are more patri-lineages than pot grounds, lineage fission may have occurred faster than fresh pot grounds could be started. The younger patrilineages may therefore still be using and maintaining the original pot grounds of their senior or parent patrilineages. In modern con-ditions, from fear of neglect, pots in certain pot grounds might have been transferred to the *obu*. Old pot grounds might then be built over, as seems to have happened in Ndi Edike in whose *obu* I saw rows of male pots housed in one of the two small rooms.

On the other hand, where there are more pot grounds than named patrilineages, some patrilineages have disappeared, or fusion may have occurred. In the latter case two original patri-lineages when fused are then called by one name, although they each continue to maintain their own separate lines of ancestral pots. The result is two pot grounds to what would appear in name to be only one patrilineage. This in fact is the case with Ndi Ofali 'secondary' lineage unit where two patrilineages fused under the name of Ndi Ofali, while still maintaining two separate pot grounds.

As a rule each patrilineage tries very hard to 'plant'[9] its ancestral pots in neat rows, each new pot taking its place in strict order of seniority according to the time of the death of its owner. The difficulties of really maintaining a strict order are obvious. One is that death does not come in strict order of seniority of age. Persons of about the same age die at different times. But however hard the attempt to maintain this order had been, today the action of an enlightened *ezè ezi* ('head of path') who, for the sake of preserving

[9] An ancestral pot is said to be 'planted' because by custom a shallow hole is made in the ground into which the pot is put in as in an attempt to bury it. The top half is usually exposed. In pot huts they are not usually so 'planted' but they are on the open path.

them, urges that the pots be transferred to the *obu*, may result in upsetting the original order of pots on pot grounds. A confusion never confessed to a stranger results. These are some of the reasons why any claims to a strict order of preservation of pots are, or should be, suspect.

Female Ancestral Pots

These accumulate in the matrilineal line, the same way that male ones do in the patrilineal line. It is daughters or sisters (instead of sons or brothers) who raise pots to the memory of dead mothers or sisters. And unlike male pots which one finds in the open in pot huts on village paths, female pots are kept in the bedroom of the living female elder who has taken over the responsibility of caring for them from her predecessor. She moves the pots into her bedroom after the customary ritual obligations have been met. She is supposed to plant them by her hearth in the same order in which her predecessor was also supposed to have received and planted them, adding the pot of the recently dead female adult member of her matrilineage to the number. For her and her matrilineage, to preserve and care for these pots as the predecessor had done is a grave ritual responsibility. This she accepts and carries out.

Male pots then are stationary, residence in Ohaffia being patrilocal. Female pots are not. On the contrary they move from place to place, following each female elder whose responsibility it becomes to take care of them next. Female pot trails therefore criss-cross, following each new successor into the residential patrilineage into which she has been married, or as a widow back to the patrilineage into which she was born, and out of it upon her death to her successor, who might be living in another Ohaffia village.

The pot movements in two matrilineages are charted in Figs. 12*a* and 12*b*. To start with, both diagrams show that daughter may succeed mother, and sister sister, in the responsibility of raising pots to the memories of their female ancestors and of preserving as well as caring for them. In Fig. 12*a* Nos. 1 and 2 were sisters. In the same Fig. Nos. 5 and 6, as well as Ego herself, were sisters. It probably will cause surprise that Ego's younger sister, No. 6, has a pot to her memory. It would seem, on the face of it, as if No. 6 held the eldership before her elder sister, Ego, at present the living holder of the status.[10] The answer is that she did not. What happened was that the younger sister died at a ripe old age while her sister, No. 5, was still alive and in office. Her right to a pot was because she had children who constitute an extension of the matri-lineage, and for whom she remains an ancestress. They would owe

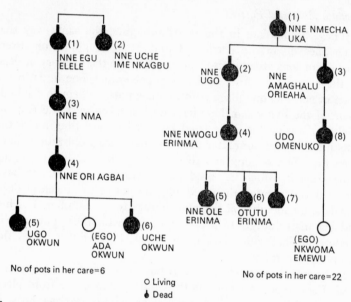

No of pots in her care=6

No of pots in her care=22

O Living
◑ Dead

FIG. 12*a*. Genealogical chart of six ancestresses whose *Udùdù* were named by Ego (ADA OKWUN) the living head of her matrilineage, who lives with her son.

FIG. 12*b*. Genealogical chart of eight ancestresses whose *Udùdù* were named by Ego (NKWOMA EMEWU) married into NDI AMECHI compound returned to NDI AJA, her own family. Ego is the living head of her matrilineage.

their spiritual well-being to her. A pot to her memory therefore would preserve the spiritual link which makes sacrificial offerings to her meaningful.

Fig. 12*b* reflects a similar pattern of rights to pot monuments at death to that which we have just explained on the basis of Fig. 12*a*. The eight women whose names were still remembered by the present living female elder, Ego, have all had pots raised to their names for the same reason which we have discussed, namely children. There is no complication in Fig. 12*b*, for none of the

[10] Ada Okwun was still alive in 1965 when I last visited Ohaffia.

ancestresses died without having held the title and status of an elder of their matrilineage first.

The living female elder is the spiritual focus of all the living members, males and females alike, of an Ohaffia matrilineage. She is the visible ancestress of them all. It is to her that they bring both their spiritual and their worldly tribulations, and expect succour. It is near her hearth and in her bedroom that the pots of their line of ancestresses find warmth, care, and devotion.

While many patrilineage pots in Ohaffia have suffered damage from exposure or from neglect, a similar fate cannot really be said to have overtaken those of the matrilineages. They still evoke stronger and deeper emotions of loyalty even today than their male counterparts do. It is in this very close-binding relationship between the living members of a matrilineage and the dead ancestresses that we see and appreciate the full implication of the Ohaffia proverb which we quoted earlier: 'Father's penis scatters, but mother's womb gathers' (*Ikpù ekpukọta ekpukọta, utù n'atu atutu*).

X

THE SOURCE OF THE OHAFFIA MATRILINEAL COMPONENT

Aberle's Theory of the Origin of Matrilineal Systems

THE Ohaffia have their own ideas about the origin of their matrilineal features. These ideas, as we have seen, are enshrined in their oral traditions. Apart from village traditions about the origins of matrilineal customs, certain lineage histories contain myths which ascribe the origins of their lineages either directly to ancestresses or indirectly to the active participation of sisters of the male lineage-founders.[1] Whatever significance one may choose to ascribe to these myths, they serve the social objective of validating the structural principle upon which crucial social relations are built. Our interest in these myths, therefore, does not derive from any historical 'truth' they purport to tell.

A modern theory of the origin of matriliny is given by Aberle.[2] It is discussed here because of its relevance to the Ohaffia case. Disagreeing with the evolutionary view of the origin of matriliny as put forward by nineteenth-century anthropological writers such as Bachofen, Maine, MacLennan, and others, Aberle substitutes an ecological explanation which is summarized as follows.

Matriliny cannot be regarded as a stage to be attained in the evolution of the human culture, or from which a culture can emerge to move to a higher one, as a monkey would to a man. If it were a stage, it would not be found in cultures which are at various levels of social organization.[3]

It should best be regarded as a specific cultural response to a particular ecological niche. Its origin lies in its function, as the growth of a thick coat of fur is a response to a cold environment.[4]

---

[1] Ndi Uyo patrilineage in Amaekpu village ascribes its origin to the aid given to the male founder of their lineage by his mother's brother's daughter (*ada nne*). A literal translation of the lineage history of the Ndi Uyo is given in the Appendix, pp. 124–7.   [2] In Schneider and Gough, 1961, pp. 655–727.

[3] Ibid., p. 658.

[4] Here, he speaks of 'red-skinned as opposed to black-skinned reptiles', as not being a stage, ibid., p. 658.

For matriliny, this function 'consists simply in assigning individuals to kinship categories by reference to descent traced through
females'.[5] For this kind of affiliation through females to develop,
the physical ecology must be such as would encourage a particular
type of subsistence economy in which the activities of the female
members dominate.[6] 'Uncomplicated horticulture'[7] provides such
an economic base, and matriliny shows an affinity for this kind of
economic system.

But not only should the niche and the level of economic organization be right, the level of social organization of the community
in which the phenomenon is to be found must also be right.
Where these minimum conditions are found, matriliny might,
but not of necessity, emerge.

The global distribution of matriliny cannot be explained by
diffusion,[8] although this can occur within contiguous territories,
as in Central Africa [and I think in the Cross River area]. Matriliny has a low frequency and its spread is uneven.[9] This uneven
spread suggests that matriliny has a narrow ecological range.[10]
Matriliny presents a variety of forms, which can be explained by
the fact of the uniqueness of each niche, although, however unique,
it must provide the minimum of conditions favourable to its
survival. The development of matrilineal types can also be
explained by past history; this too is unique for every culture, for
no two cultures can share identical historical experience even if
they live side by side. It can therefore be said that ecology provides
the scope for survival but that the difference of historical experience promotes the development of matrilineal types. The Bantu
matrilineal cluster in Central Africa, for example, could be
explained by diffusion but their different types could be explained
by their unique social experiences.

Now what evidence there is also suggests that matriliny tends
to favour certain types of economic systems whose productive
capacities may not exceed certain levels.[11] Such economic systems
must be subsistence economies which would demand minimum
mobility.[12] Matriliny is rare where pastoral and such extractive
economic activities as fishing, hunting, and gathering are dominant,
although exceptions occur in certain types of fishing economy.

[5] Aberle, op. cit., p. 656. [6] Ibid., p. 670. [7] Ibid., p. 679.
[8] Ibid., p. 659. [9] Ibid., pp. 663–4. [10] Ibid., p. 670.
[11] Ibid., pp. 670 and 691–2. [12] Ibid., pp. 664 and 691.

Extractive economic activities, whether at the subsistence or at a highly mechanized level, are on the whole unsettling. Like pastoral herding, they require constant movement which gathering and hunting impose on communities who live by them. In these communities, division of labour is heavily weighted in favour of the male members whose rights also seem to be paramount. There matrilineal elements would either be absent or submerged. Matriliny would also be absent in modern industrial cultures because of their high degree of complex political and social organization and their high degree of individuation.

These being unfavourable environments for the development or survival of matriliny, we are left with one type of economic system which is not only subsistence but non-extractive. This is subsistence agriculture. But subsistence agriculture is in itself a complex. There are certain types of it that are inimical to matriliny, such as the types in which the plough is used, with the burden of long and heavy labour devolving either upon draught animal 'domesticates', mainly oxen, or upon the menfolk. It happens that in the vast majority of areas where the plough and the oxen or other large domestic animals are used for agriculture, or where farming is heavily aided by irrigation, matriliny is absent or rare.

Forest farming is also not conducive to matrilineal cultures, and it is to be suspected that if matriliny is found in a forest area the explanation would lie in recent migration of the people who must have carried the phenomenon with them into such an environment.[13] Most favourable to matriliny are the types of subsistence agriculture carried on in areas marginal to forest lands: areas of forest vegetation transitional to savanna and the jungle, the tropical orchard bush where vegetation cover is light, and warm temperate lands where the burden of farm work is not so heavy as to rule out the use of the labour of the womenfolk. In such conditions it would appear that men and women alike could fairly easily meet the demands of farm work without the need for elaborate farm implements like the plough, or irrigation techniques. This bias of matriliny for marginal forest lands and for fair division of labour in subsistence farming is only a trend favouring its growth and perpetuation.

There is also some association between matriliny and certain levels of political organization. It is found more commonly in

[13] Aberle, op. cit., p. 668.

segmentary political systems, than in 'state-like' political systems, and less so in large modern and highly centralized states with high economic productivity than in 'state-like' systems. Matriliny also tends to shy away from highly stratified communities, such as caste communities, or communities where the factor of economic surplus would create privileged groups who would control both the means of production and the wealth thus produced. Where the contrary is the case, as in Assam in India, the explanation would be that a recent migration of a 'matrilineal' community to a new social environment where the caste system had earlier become established must have occurred. But it is also likely that matriliny would not survive for long under such a rigid social environment.

Matriliny seems to favour non-exogamous localized communities in which the choice of wives within them may not be prohibited by the rigid taboo of exogamy and in which endogamy may be permissible but may not be the rule among patrilineage groups. [All this, as we have seen, is true of the Ohaffia Ibo.]

The explanation for exceptions of fishing communities in which matriliny occurs contrary to the view put forward here, such as for example the North American Indian fishing communities, may lie in the type of fish caught. In such areas the fish are salmon. These go downstream at the proper season in great shoals; catching them therefore is comparable to farm harvesting which would demand minimum mobility, not comparable at all to the kind occasioned by hunting or gathering. The same explanation would hold for lake fishing of some Bantu 'matrilineal' groups which again requires minimum mobility.

Aberle's theoretical position may crudely be summed up thus: that matriliny would develop in communities with a simple horticultural base with women doing the agricultural labour rather than in the largest political units based on high agricultural productivity and at the highest level of industrial organization and productivity.[14]

His theoretical position, as abridged, is essentially conjectural no less than were the views of the anthropological writers of the nineteenth century which he has rejected on evolutionary rather than on conjectural grounds. He does what they did, which is to take a look at the data that the world distribution of the phenomenon of matriliny provides, noting the peculiarities of both

[14] Aberle, op. cit., p. 670.

the ecological and the social environments in which various forms of matrilineal systems thrive. Having assessed these data, he takes a theoretical position on the possible conditions which might have encouraged the rise of matriliny. He projects these conditions into the past to explain the possible origin of the phenomenon.

Cases such as those of the Bantu or the Assam matrilineal systems which do not deviate too far from the ideal conditions which he has set up, but which nevertheless cannot be neatly explained by his theory, he explains by the historical event of a recent migration. Thus he seems able to explain the source of each known case of matriliny by his two-in-one theory. Even so his theoretical position remains conjectural in that it is still the explanation of the past by the projection of the present into it. This, as I have said, in no way differs from the conjectural positions of the anthropological writers of the past century, except that while most of them tried to explain social origins within the framework of biological concepts, such as evolution, Aberle does so in terms of ecology, or when convenient, of history. So the verdict upon Aberle's view must be that, however plausible it might seem, the case has not been proved.

However, the Ohaffia and the environment in which they live fit so neatly into many of Aberle's theoretical requirements, that, but for other reasons, one would be tempted to explain the origin of Ohaffia 'matriliny' in terms of his adaptive theory. For, as we have shown, Ohaffia country lies in a transitional vegetation zone between savanna and forest. Moreover, the Ohaffia themselves have a simple horticultural economic base and a segmentary form of political organization. They live in a social environment which was, until recently, in a state of turmoil. This appears to have imposed the responsibility of territorial defence and expansion upon the menfolk, and to have transferred the burden of food production to the womenfolk, although the Ohaffia claim that they have always been a warrior community.

Ohaffia Matriliny Borrowed

However, there are good reasons for the view that the Ohaffia are more likely to be borrowers rather than the originators of their matrilineal features. The Ohaffia were latecomers to their present environment. To the east of their country live numerous groups of peoples, all of them speakers of the 'Ekoid' or 'Bantoid' languages and in whose social systems are to be found distinct clusters of matrilineal traits. These communities seemed to have settled earlier than the Ohaffia in the middle Cross River area and they are the same people to whom Forde and Jones referred when they spoke of the 'semi-Bantu peoples east of the Cross River, such as the Yakö and Agwa' agune', with whom the Ohaffia, Abiriba, and Abam share many cultural features.[15]

Further evidence favouring the likelihood of borrowing lies in the fact that although the Cross River 'semi-Bantu' peoples now live mainly on the eastern bank of the river, they once settled on its western bank, in what today is largely Ibo territory; this was before the Ibo moved in from the west to occupy the country. It is reasonable to suppose that even during the period of turmoil which marked the confrontation between the Abam and the 'semi-Bantu' groups, much mixing must have occurred. In possessing the land, the immigrant Ohaffia group may also have absorbed some remnants of the aboriginal groups as well as their customs.[16] The village of Ihenta, which was formerly not part of Ohaffia but now is, serves as an example of what might have occurred. The mixed population types of the Ohaffia would seem to indicate that absorption had occurred, just as certain non-Ibo cultural traits, such as answering to names of non-Ibo origin, also do. As simple as it is, this is the case for the view that the Ohaffia must have borrowed their matrilineal features from their neighbours east of the Cross River.

It remains to show that some of the peoples east of the Cross River about whom we have any knowledge[17] do have matrilineal traits in their cultures. These traits appear in various forms, but the relationship with the patrilineal traits is not stable. For example, among the Yakö who are members of this cluster, rules governing the right to inherit lands recognize the patrilineal line only, although in the same group members of the 'matrilineal kinship should take precedence over patrilineal in the inheritance of all transferable wealth, especially livestock and currency, in the receipt of marriage payments made to a woman's brother at her marriage . . .'.[18] It is the Yakö who say, as the Ohaffia do, that

---

[15] Forde and Jones, 1950, p. 55.

[16] See Harris, 1962, p. 48, for similar references to absorption of this sort.

[17] Apart from Professor Forde's intensive study of the Yakö, still very little is known about most of the communities under reference.

[18] Forde, 1964, p. 96.

'a man eats in his *kepun* [patrilineage] but inherits in his *lejima* [matriclan].'[19] But Forde also notes that there is now a determination to flout such matrilineal rights as still exist among the Yakö.[20] This seems to suggest that change is taking place, for he also adds that 'formerly marriage within the matriclan was strongly disapproved'.[21]

Although, like the Yakö, the Mbembe, who are neighbours to the Yakö and live east of them, '. . . recognize double unilineal descent . . . the Mbembe system differs considerably in detail from that of the Yako'.[22] Also, in the same area, we find the Agoi recognizing rights whereby lands are passed down matrilineally as well as patrilineally. Similar reversals of rights are to be found too in rules governing marriage practices among these same peoples. The Yakö patriclan, for instance, is 'strictly exogamous'.[23] By the Mbembe, in contrast, 'marriages within the patriclan are certainly not prohibited and may even be favoured',[24] just as in Ohaffia.

The important thing to note is that whatever the rights are, in the Cross River and neighbouring areas they flow through both patrilineal and matrilineal lines of descent but by no means in equal measures in the various groups referred to.

[19] Forde, op. cit., p. 96.   [20] Ibid., p. 97.   [21] Ibid., pp. 105–6.
[22] Harris, 1962, p. 40.   [23] Ibid., p. 95.   [24] Ibid., p. 40.

XI

CONCLUSION

Ohaffia Kinship as a Double-Descent System

TWO contrasting social systems emerge from the cultural differences that have been shown to exist between the Ohaffia and the general Ibo. The system which most Ibo have has been termed patrilineal. That of the Ohaffia Ibo has been put by Goody in the same category as the double descent systems of the Yakö and the Lo Dagaba.[1] I shall show that there are actually one or two differences. Four theoretical criteria were used by Goody in his classification: (i) that a double descent system should have two descent groups, each group to be known and called by a technical term as well as by a name; the term and the name should be indigenous (Goody,* Schneider*); (ii) that each of the two descent groups should be a 'corporation', i.e. should be a property-owning and property-inheriting group (Forde,* Goody,* Maine,* Radcliffe-Brown,* Schneider*); (iii) that each of the two descent groups in a double descent system should, in principle, be localized; but where they are dispersed they should live close enough to be able to meet and take decisions and be able to act as a group, usually under a head. The existence of a head would imply some degree of ranking or 'pyramidal' structuring in the group (Durkheim,* Radcliffe-Brown,* Weber*); (iv) finally, that each of the two descent groups should be strictly exogamous (Forde,* Goody,* Schneider*).

Goody has also suggested the minimum number of criteria for a social system to be called a double descent system. This minimum is two, namely 'double clanship' and 'double inheritance', (iv) and (ii) above. 'Double clanship' requires that each of the two descent groups should be exogamous, while 'double inheritance' implies that each descent group should be able to own and transmit property in the line.

* Authors who expressed the same view.

[1] Goody, J., 'The Classification of Double Descent', *Current Anthropology*, ii, No. 1 (Feb. 1961), 3–25.

The Yakö have been shown by Forde to have both 'double clanship' and 'double inheritance'. Both the patrilineage and the matrilineage in Yakö are strictly exogamous and both are property-holding and property-transmitting corporations. The Yakö patrilineage also has both an indigenous technical term (*kepun*) and a name which belonged as a rule to the original founder of the patrilineage. The Yakö matrilineage too is called by a technical term (*lejima*) and is named after its ancestress. The Yakö patrilineage is invariably localized, whereas the members of the matrilineage, although generally dispersed, are known to meet under a recognized head to take decisions or carry them out. Thus the Yakö, by the above criteria, have been shown to have two full descent groups, one patrilineal, one matrilineal, and therefore can be appropriately classified as having a 'full' double descent system.[2]

The Lo Dagaba, as shown by Goody, have a double descent system like the Yakö. They have named exogamous patrilineages and matrilineages. The patrilineage is also known by an indigenous term (*sāā per*),[3] and the matrilineage by the term *ma per*.[4] Both the Lo Dagaba patrilineage and the matrilineage are property-owning and property-inheriting corporations. Members of the Lo Dagaba descent groups of either category meet to take decisions and can execute them in common action. The patrilineage is localized because it is the residential unit but the matrilineage is dispersed. So, like the Yakö, the Lo Dagaba can be said to have a double descent system.

The Ohaffia descent system differs from those of the Yakö and the Lo Dagaba. The extent of this difference can be seen from the extent to which the four criteria which Goody suggests apply to the Ohaffia. With regard to the first of these criteria, that concerning the ownership of a technical term and a personal name, both the patrilineage and the matrilineage in Ohaffia have these. *Umudi* is the term for patrilineage, as we have already noted, and *umudi* also bears the personal name of the ancestor of the patrilineage, such as *Ukpọla* in Fig. 9. The matrilineage is technically termed *ikwu*, and each matrilineage has its personal name, such as *Eke Uke*, the name of Ego's matrilineage in Fig. 9.

Unlike the Yakö and the Lo Dagaba systems, the matrilineage

---

[2] Goody, 1961, p. 12.
[3] J. Goody, *Death, Property, and the Ancestors*, London, 1959, p. 102.
[4] Ibid., p. 102.

in the Ohaffia system is the main corporation, i.e. the property-owning and property-transmitting group. In this connection it has earlier been pointed out that a male member of an Ohaffia patrilineage would rather add to the lands of his own matrilineage than to those of his patrilineage. Nevertheless, members of a patrilineage transmit rights in residential lands (*èzi*) patrilineally; and where the patrilineage has lands (these are usually pledged or *ukwuzi* lands), the right to use these is also patrilineally inherited by the group. Unbuilt-on lands as well as estates acquired by individuals are matrilineally inherited throughout Ohaffia.

The residential group is the patrilineage. Therefore, by the third criterion, it is the matrilineage that is dispersed, but its members, as we have seen, are strongly bound together not only by strict rules of exogamy and the ownership of landed property and its resources but also by a strong emotional attachment to the ancestral pots (*ududu*) of a long line of ancestresses which are left in the care of the head of the matrilineage.

The Ohaffia matrilineage exhibits its dominance in the Ohaffia social system by the strict rule of exogamy which precludes marriage among its members. But, unlike in the Yakö and the Lo Dagaba and most Ibo, the patrilineage in Ohaffia is non-exogamous. Now to sum up, not only is the Ohaffia matrilineage the main property-owning and inheriting group, it is also the only exogamous group; the patrilineage is non-exogamous and not the main property-owning or property-inheriting group, quite unlike its counterpart in Yakö and Lo Dagaba.

If then the Ohaffia descent system is to be classified as one of double descent, it must also be made clear that matrilineal elements are dominant in the system. As suggested by P. E. de Josselin de Jong[5] in his comments on Goody's classification, it will not be sufficient merely to say that a descent system is one of double descent, for in few societies, if any, are the essential factors involved neatly balanced between the male and the female lines. If Goody's own classification scheme has to be adopted, using both his minimum criteria (of which exogamy is one), then the Ohaffia should strictly go with the Ashanti who are classified by Goody as a matrilineal system with named complementary agnatic groups. The Ohaffia cannot in any event be grouped, as Goody

[5] In Goody, 1961, p. 14.

has done,[6] with the Yakö or with the Lo Dagaba without a firm note on the dominance of matrilineality in their system.

The Ohaffia System and Social Change

It remains to show whether there have been shifts indicating any fundamental change in the Ohaffia descent system as described, particularly with regard to the rules of inheritance. From what the Ohaffia themselves say, they now seem to resent their rule of inheritance which channels practically all property through the matrilineal line. And they speak rather disapprovingly of the way members of the matrilineage 'sweep clean' the house of a deceased relative when they come to lay claim to his property.

In cases where the claims of a matrilineage lie outside Ohaffia such claims will need to be backed by the certification of the court in Ohaffia, as we have noted in an earlier chapter. This means that the custom of matrilineal inheritance in Ohaffia enjoys a modern legal sanction provided by the Government of the region.

The custom can only be worsted in one of two ways, by a wealthy Ohaffia father who wants to avoid the complete transfer of his wealth to a sister's son. He can try while still living to provide as fully as possible for his sons. He can give a portion of his wealth to give them a start in life, usually in trade or in farming. If the latter, he can provide them with their first yam seeds in an initiation ritual known as *igwa ọba* ('starting a barn'). He may also provide the marriage payment. Today these have been replaced by a different kind of asset. Now fathers prefer to educate their children, to give them what no matrilineage can take away, namely, knowledge and education with all that these can bestow upon their possessor. An Ohaffia father, provided his children are able, would help them on to any level of education which his means can provide. Whatever else is given to a son or daughter by a father during his own lifetime, this the matrilineage cannot take away.[7]

Alternatively, especially in respect of bought lands and estates such as plantation farms, a father may apportion parts of these to his sons, leaving the rest to his matrilineage. But this must be done before he dies and in the presence of witnesses usually from his own matrilineage, otherwise his sons would lose all claims to them.

[6] In Goody, 1961, p. 14.
[7] A. K. Uche, *Customs and Practices in Ohaffia*, Aba, Nigeria, 1960, pp. 39–40.

A recent shift in the inheritance of property is towards the apportionment of these, especially valuable property, before the death of the owner. But the shift should by no means be regarded as constituting a legal testament which 'is still the exception rather than the rule in most areas'[8] in Eastern Nigeria.

In other respects in which matrilineal rules affect succession, little change has occurred. But the direction seems clear. While the secular headship of a matrilineage which carries the responsibility for protecting the property and the resources of the matrilineage will clearly remain in the matrilineal line, the ritual headship vested in the female head of the matrilineage is likely to vanish as more and more Ohaffia females (in whom lies the hope of perpetuating the office) become better educated or come to accept the Christian faith. Then the dead will have lost their traditional hold upon the hearts of their living daughters and sons, who will now have to learn to remember and honour their ancestors no longer through the vehicle of old beliefs and old values but through their Christian substitutes. Then the sacred pots will vanish with the warmth of the traditional bedroom fire, and the ancient devotion that had once sustained them and their guardians.

---

[8] E. W. Ardener, 'A Note on Intestate Succession in Parts of Nigeria and Cameroon', unpublished manuscript, West Cameroon Archives, Buea, Cameroon.

APPENDIX

Akiko bayere umu nna
History of a patrilineage (minimal segment)

Source: Ofia Idika's Diary, Dated 12 July 1926, recopied
11 Sept. 1932.*

Ibo	*English*
Ayi nuru na mgbe ndi ochie sina obu Aja Iyi supere ezi ndi Uyo.	We heard that in times of old it was Aja Iyi who cleared the path of Uyo patrilineage.
Aja Iyi ahu buru onye ikwu umu Ibe Obobi.	The said Aja Iyi was a man from Ibe Obobi matrilineage.
Ezi ahu n'adakari ya oku.	The said path was for him too hot.
Ya we resiya Okwu.	He then sold it to Okwu.
Okwu we susia ezi ahu wukwasi ya ulo ya.	Okwu then cleared the path and built on it his house.
Mbe ogara igbara aja na nke otu dibia, dibia ahu gwa ya ka okporo adanneya nwayi la n'ezi ahu.	When he went to a diviner, the said diviner advised him to take the eldest daughter of his mother's 'brother' back to the path.
Aha adanneya nwayi ahu buru Afonta Nnachi.	The name of the daughter of his mother's 'brother' was Afonta Nnachi.
Ukpaize bukwa onye Ibe Obobi na nna ndi Odike,	Ukpaize (who) was a man from Ibe Obobi (matrilineage) but of Odike patrilineage,
gwa Uyo Ukpai nwaya ka olaku Okwu nwaneya n'ezi ohuru ahu.	told Uyo Ukpai his son to live with Okwu his 'brother' in the said new path.
Na nwa mgbe Okwu nwua.	Shortly after Okwu died.
Uyo Ukpai biri n'ebe ahu mua Odo Uyo.	Uyo Ukpai stayed on there (and) begat Odo Uyo.
Mbe Odo Uyo tuliri,	When Odo Uyo grew up,
Uyo Ukpai bu nnaya nwukwa.	Uyo Ukpai his father died.
Mgbe ahu Odo Uyo enwegh ike ichekota aku nnaya.	But then Odo Uyo could not take care of his father's wealth.
Site na nka,	Because of this,

* The word division in the Ibo portion of this document does not always follow strict conventions, and I have not amended this.

Ibo	*English*
ya agbaga Asaga ikporo Amogu Awa bu nwanne-nnaya ka obia buru onye isi n'ikwu ahu.	he hastened to Asaga to take Amogu Awa his father's 'brother' to come to be head of that matrilineage.
Mgbe oruru n'Asaga,	When he reached Asaga,
y'ahu sina Amogu Awa lukwara Ole Ukpai Anya bu oru nwanneya ochie Odo gbara.	he saw that Amogu Awa had married Ole Ukpai Anya the slave his elder 'brother' Odo had acquired.
Odo kporo Amogu na nwie ya na Nwoke Amogu nwa ha lua.	Odo took Amogu and his wife and Nwoke Amogu their child home.
Ha we biri n'ezi Ndi Ngwoke n'erikwa ji n'ubochi Afo dika Asaga.	They then lived in the path of Ngwoke patrilineage and adopted Afo day as the day for the rite of yam-eating like the Asaga.
Ole Ukpai Anya mukwara Amogu nwa abua bu Kalu Amogu na Ugoha Amogu bu nwayi.	Ole Ukpai Anya had for Amogu two children who were Kalu Amogu and Ugoha Amogu a daughter.
Okewu Obuba Odike lua Ugoha Amogu.	Okewu Obuba Odike married Ugoha Amogu.
Ugoha murua ya Obuba Okewa na Eke Okewu.	Ugoha bore him Obuba Okewu and Eke Okewu.
Obuba na Eke Okewu musia ezi ndi Okewu.	Obuba and Eke Okewu greatly increased the patrilineage of Okewu.
Uyo Ukpai luda adanne nnaya bu Ukpaize.	Uyo Ukpai married his father's sister's daughter named Ukpaize.
Uyo Ukpai mua Odo Uyo.	Uyo Ukpai begat Odo Uyo.
Odo Uyo mua Okoronkwo-Odo Uyo.	Odo Uyo begat Odo Okoronkwo-Odo Uyo.
Odo Okoronkwo mua Nnoke Odo.	Odo Okoronkwo begat Nnoke Odo.
Nnoke Odo mua Odo Nnoke.	Nnoke Odo begat Odo Nnoke.
Odo Nnoke mua Mba Nnoke na Akaji Nnoke.	Odo Nnoke begat Mba Nnoke and Akaji Nnoke.
Mba Nnoke mua Ibeke Nnoke na Ebi Nnoke.	Mba Nnoke begat Ibeke Nnoke and Ebi Nnoke.
Akaji Nnoke mua Nnoke Akaji.	Akaji Nnoke begat Nnoke Akaji.
Nnoke Akaji mua Udonsi Nnoke.	Nnoke Akaji begat Udonsi Nnoke.

Ibo	*English*
Chima Uduma Ezichi buru onye ikwu ndi Ibe Obobi.	Chima Uduma Ezichi was a man from Ibe Obobi matrilineage.
Ya lua adanne Umu Atum.	He married from Umu Atum (mother's patrilineage).
Adanne Umu Atum ahu buru oru.	The woman so married was a slave.
Ya murua Chima otutu umuntakiri.	She bore Chima very many children.
Dika uma ndi ochie diri mgbe ahu,	According to the custom of those olden days,
oburu na iluru oru nwayi	if you married a slave woman,
ya mua otutu umu ndiya n'acho ikpokwara ya,	and she bore very many children and her people wanted her back,
ha ga ahapu otu onye nyekwa nnaya.	they should leave one only of the children for the father.
Umu Atum mere otu ahu nye Chima mgbe ha kpokwara adanne ha bu nwie Chima.	Umu Atum did that to Chima when they took '*adanne*' the wife of Chima back.
Nwanta nke ahu ha nyere Chima buru Orioka Chima.	The child they gave Chima was Orioka Chima.
Orioka Chima achogh ibi n'ebe nnaya Chima.	Orioka Chima did not wish to live with her father Chima.
Ya mere ka oji gbakukwara umu nneya n'Abiriba.	This was why she ran to her brothers and sisters at Abiriba.
Mbe obiri n'Abiriba ha yepuru ya ime nwa agbogho,	At Abiriba where she lived she was made pregnant (young and unmarried),
ya mua Ukwa Ori.	she bore Ukwa Ori.
Ihe mere ha ji gua ya Ukwa Ori bu amagh nnaya.	Why the child was named Ukwa Ori was because its father was not known.
Aha anakpo nwa di otu ahu bu Nwa-Uga-da-muga.	The name given to such a child is 'Nwa-Uga-da-muga'.
Mgbe Orioka Chima n'acho ilahachikwa n'ebe nnaya,	When Orioka decided to return to her father,
ya lagasa uzo ndi Nku,	she travelled through Ndi Nku,
mbe ahu Iroha Ogwe hure ya yekwa ya ime ozo.	there Iroha Ogwe caught and made her pregnant again.
Ya mua nwa-agbogho anakpo Mburu Iroha.	She bore a young woman named Mburu Iroha.
Mburu bu aha aguruya site n'okeenkwa nke onebundere ndi ichin.	She was named Mburu because of the special dance she danced for elders.

Ibo	*English*
Ezi aha ya buru Ọnu Irọha.	Her real name was Ọnu Iroha.
Mgbe Odo Uyọ huru si ọburu adanne nwayi nnaya,	When Odo Uyọ discovered that she was the daughter of his father's wife,
ya we lukwara ya.	he married her.
Ya murua Odo Uyọ nwa nwayi bu Ukọma Odo.	She bore Odo Uyọ a daughter named Ukọma Odo.
Mgbe Odo Uyọ nwuru Ukọma we n'eso nneya eje na Ntakpu nka Ibe Okon Alinta bu *uzi* nneya igbari ukpara.	When Odo Uyọ died Ukọma began going with his mother to hunt grass-hoppers in *Ntakpu* bush owned by his mother's lover named Ibe Okon Alinta.
Ndi nyere Ibe Okon ala ahu bu Umu Ubia ndi Asaga.	Those who gave Ibe Okon the bush were Umu Ubia of Asaga.

Ala nka ha napuru ayi
(Bush taken away from us)

1. Otutu ndi Odo
2. Otutu obuba ndu
3. Nde ndi Odo
4. Orua ndi Odo
5. Ali Enyi

Ala nka agbara ibe
(Bush pledged)

1. Ali Enyi
2. Otutu Uzo Ezi

BIBLIOGRAPHY

ABERLE, D. F., 1961, 'Matrilineal Descent in Cross-cultural Perspective', in *Matrilineal Kinship*, by D. M. Schneider and K. Gough, Berkeley and Los Angeles, Cal., pp. 655–727.

ARDENER, E. W., 1954, 'The Kinship Terminology of a Group of Southern Ibo', *Africa*, xxiv. 85–99.

—— 1959, 'Lineage and Locality among the Mba-Ise Ibo', *Africa*, xxix. 113–32.

—— 'A Note on Intestate Succession in Parts of Nigeria and Cameroon', unpublished manuscript, West Cameroon Archives, Buea, Cameroon.

—— 1962, *Divorce and Fertility*, London.

—— 1968, 'Documentary and Linguistic Evidence for the Rise of the Trading Polities between Rio Del Rey and Cameroons, 1500–1650', *History and Social Anthropology*, A.S.A. Monograph No. 7, London.

BASDEN, G. T., 1938, *The Niger Ibos*, London.

BAUMANN, H., 1928, 'Division of Work according to Sex in African Hoe Culture', *Africa*, i. 389–99.

BECROFT, Capt., 1841, 'On Benin and the Upper Course of the River Quorra, or Niger', as communicated by Robert Jamieson in the *Journal of the Royal Geographical Society of London*, xi. 189–90.

BRIFFAULT, R., 1959, *The Mothers*, London, as abridged by G. R. Taylor.

BROWN, P., 1951, 'Patterns of Authority in West Africa', *Africa*, xxi. 261–78.

DALZIEL, J. M., 1948, *The Useful Plants of West Tropical Africa*, London, 1948.

District Court Grade A Record Book, No. 4/60, Ebem, 1965.

ELUWA, B. O. N., 'Ado N'idu', unpublished manuscript.

EVANS-PRITCHARD, E. E., 1951, *Social Anthropology*, London.

FORDE, D., 1964, *Yakö Studies*, London.

—— and JONES, G. I., 1950, *The Ibo and Ibibio-speaking Peoples of South-Eastern Nigeria*, London.

FORTES, M., 1953, 'The Structure of Unilineal Descent Groups', *American Anthropologist*, lv. 17–41.

—— and EVANS-PRITCHARD, E., 1940, *African Political Systems*, London.

—— 1950, *African System of Kinship and Marriage*, London.

FOX, R., 1967, *Kinship and Marriage*, Harmondsworth.

GLUCKMAN, M., 1950, 'Kinship and Marriage among The Lozi of Northern Rhodesia and the Zulu of Natal', in *African Systems of Kinship and Marriage*, ed. Radcliffe-Brown, A. R., and Forde, D., London, pp. 166–206.

GOODY, J., 1959, *Death, Property, and the Ancestors*, London.

—— 1959a, 'Mother's Brother and Sister's Son in West Africa', *Journal of the Royal Anthropological Institute*, lxxxix. 61–88.

—— 1961, 'The Classification of Double Descent', *Current Anthropology*, ii, No. 1, pp. 3–25.

GREEN, M. M., 1941, *Land Tenure in an Ibo Village*, London.

—— 1947, *Ibo Village Affairs*, London.

GREENBERG, J. H., 1963, *Languages of Africa*, The Hague.

HARRIS, J. S., 1943, 'Papers on the Economic Aspect of Life among the Ozuitem Ibo', *Africa*, xiv. 12–23.

HARRIS, R., 1962, 'The Influence of Ecological Factors and External Relations on the Mbembe Tribes of South-east Nigeria', *Africa*, xxxii. 38–52.

HART, A. K., 1964, *Report of the Inquiry into the Dispute over Obongship of Calabar*, Official Document, No. 17, Government Printer, Enugu, Eastern Nigeria.

HARTLAND, E. SIDNEY, 1917, 'Matrilineal Kinship and the Question of its Priority', *Memoirs of the American Anthropological Association*, iv. 1–87.

HODGEN, M. T., 1964, *Early Anthropology in the Sixteenth and Seventeenth Centuries*, Philadelphia, Pa.

HORTON, W. R. G., 1954, 'The *Ohu* System of Slavery in a Northern Ibo Village-group', *Africa*, xxiv. 311–36.

'Idika's Diary', 1926 (recopied 1932), Unpublished manuscript.

IRVINE, F. R., 1934, *A Text-book of West African Agriculture, Soils, and Crops*, London.

JONES, G. I., 1949, 'Dual Organization in Ibo Social Structure', *Africa*, xix. 150–6.

—— 1961, 'Ecology and Social Structure among the North Eastern Ibo', *Africa*, xxxi. 117–34.

—— 1962, 'Ibo Age Organization, with Special Reference to the Cross River and North-Eastern Ibo', *Journal of the Royal Anthropological Institute*, xcii. 191–211.

KABERRY, P. M., 1967, 'The Plasticity of New Guinea Kinship', in Freedman, M. (ed.), *Social Organization: Essays Presented to R. Firth*, London, pp. 105–23.

KARLSSON, G., 1963, 'On Mate Selection', in *Family and Marriage*, ed. Mogey, J., Leiden, pp. 91–123.

KITSON, A. E., 1913, 'Southern Nigeria: Some Considerations of its Structure, People and Natural History', *Geographical Journal*, xli. 16–38.

KOELLE, the Revd. S. W., 1854, *Polyglotta Africana*, London.

LÉVI-STRAUSS, C., 1963, *Structural Anthropology*, London.

LITTLE, K. L., 1951, *The Mende of Sierra Leone*, London.
—— 1965, 'The Political Function of the Poro', Part I, *Africa*, xxxv. 349–65.
—— 1966, 'The Political Function of the Poro', Part II, *Africa*, xxxvi. 62–72.
LOWIE, R. H., 1919, 'Matrilineal Complex', University of California Publication in *American Archaeology and Ethnology*, xvi, No. 2, pp. 29–45.
—— 1937, *The History of Ethnographic Theory*, London.
—— 1949, 'Das Mutterrecht' (A Review), *American Anthropologist*, li. 628–9.
MACALISTER, D. A., 1902, 'The Aro Country, Southern Nigeria', *Scottish Geographical Magazine*, xviii. 631–7.
MALINOWSKI, B., 1929, *The Sexual Life of Savages*, London.
MEEK, C. K., 1937, *Law and Authority in a Nigerian Tribe*, London.
MIDDLETON, J. and TAIT, D. (eds.), 1958, *Tribes Without Rulers*, London.
MOCKLER-FERRYMAN, Lt.-Col. A. F., 1901, 'British Nigeria', *Journal of African Society*, i. 160–73.
MORGAN, W. B., and MOSS, R. P., 1965, 'Savanna and Forest in Western Nigeria', *Africa*, xxxv. 286–94.
MORTON-WILLIAMS, P., 1960, 'The Yoruba Ogboni Cult in Oyo', *Africa*, xxx. 362–74.
MURDOCK, G. P., 1940, 'Double Descent', *American Anthropologist*, xlii. 555–61.
National Archives, Enugu, Eastern Nigeria:
Intelligence Report on Ohaffia Clan, 1931.
Intelligence Report on Ebem Court Area, Ohaffia Clan, File 94/1931A.
Resident's Covering Report, Ref. No. OW. 1087/36 of 28 Apr. 1933.
Memorandum, by J. C. Mayne, Ref. No. 873/31, 22 Jan. 1934.
Communications between the Secretary, Southern Provinces, Enugu, Ref. No. 10411/2, Jan. 1934, and the Chief Secretary, Lagos, Ref. No. 29196, 13 Mar. 1934, and May 1934.
Intelligence Report on the Qua Clan, File No. 8965A.
National Library, Enugu, Eastern Nigeria: *The 1959 Federal Election Register of Electors* (Nigeria), Constituency No. 259, Bendè East, Section 1, Sub-unit A, AMAUKWU-KWA and NDI ERIM (Abiriba Local Council, Ward No. 1).
Report of the Constituency Delimitation Commission, 1964.
NEEDHAM, R., 1962, *Structure and Sentiment*, Chicago, Ill.
—— 1966, *Age, Category, and Descent* (*Bijdragen*), S'Gravenhage.
RADCLIFFE-BROWN, A. R., 'Mother's Brother in South Africa', *South African Journal of Science*, xxi. 542–55.
READER, D. H., 1964, 'A Survey of Categories of Economic Activities Among the Peoples of Africa', *Africa*, xxxiv. 28–45.

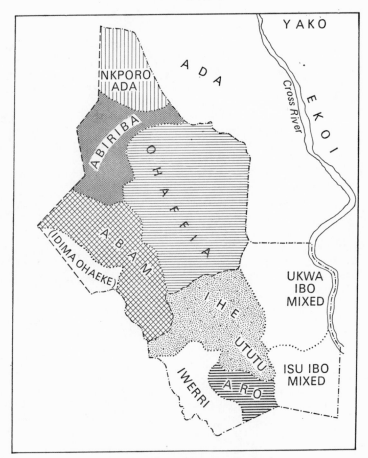

MAP 4. The Cross River Ibo Territories

RECLUS, E., *Primitive Folk*, London (not dated).

Report of the Constituency Delimitation Commission, Government Printer, Lagos, 1958.

REYFISCH, F., 1960, 'The Dynamics of Multilineality on the Mambila Plateau', *Africa*, xxx. 246–61.

RICHARDS, A. I., 1934, 'Mother-right among the Central Bantu', in *Essays Presented to C. G. Seligman*, ed. Evans-Pritchard, E. E., London, pp. 267–80.

—— 1950, 'Some Types of Family Structure Among the Central Bantu', in *African Systems of Kinship and Marriage*, ed. Radcliffe-Brown, A. F., and Forde, D., London, pp. 207–51.

ROSE, H. J., 1911, 'On the Alleged Evidence of Mother-right in Early Greece', *Folklore*, xxii. 277–91.

SCHAPERA, I., 1957, 'Marriage of near Kin among the Tswana', *Africa*, xxvii. 139–59.

SCHEFFLER, H. W., 1966, 'Ancestor Worship in Anthropology: Or, Observations on Descent and Descent Groups', *Current Anthropology*, vii. 541–51.

SCHNEIDER, D. M., and GOUGH, K., 1961, *Matrilineal Kinship*, Berkeley and Los Angeles, Cal.

SMITH, S. R., 1929, 'The Ibo People', Vols. i and ii, unpublished manuscript, Pitt Rivers Museum, Oxford.

Studies in the Laws of Succession in Nigeria: Essays Edited with an Introductory Chapter by DERRET, J. D. M., London, 1965.

TALBOT, P. A., 1926, *The Peoples of Southern Nigeria*, London, 1926.

UCHE, K. A., 1960, *Custom and Practices in Ohaffia*, Aba.

UCHENDU, V. C., 1965, *The Igbo of Southeast Nigeria*, New York.

WALKER, Capt. B. J., 1876, 'Notes of a Visit, in May 1875, to the Old Calabar and Qua Rivers, the Ekoi Country and the Qua Rapids', *Proceedings of the Royal Geographical Society*, xx. 224–30.

GENERAL INDEX